FALL '99
use selected
parts to start
year # 6.
LET'S REVIEW
SOME BASICS!!

Umc
Ga. Fk.
7/98

HANDBELL HELPER

A Guide for Beginning Directors and Choirs

Martha Lynn Thompson

D1157883

Abingdon Press
Nashville

HANDBELL HELPER
A Guide for Beginning Directors
and Choirs

Copyright © 1996 by Abingdon Press

This book is printed on acid-free, recycled paper.

ISBN 0-687-02086-7

Scripture quotations noted KJV are from the King James Version of the Bible.

96 97 98 99 00 01 02 03 04 05 — 10 9 8 7 6 5 4 3 2 1

MANUFACTURED IN THE UNITED STATES OF AMERICA

Contents

Preface

"We have some money in the memorial fund that I'd like to spend on the music program. What would you like to buy?" the superintendent asked.

"Well, we've heard that handbells are the coming thing. Why don't we buy a set?" we answered naïvely.

"Fine! Order a set and have them here in three weeks," he replied.

The year was 1966. The place was the Methodist Children's Home in Little Rock, Arkansas, and this was our introduction to the wonderful world of handbell ringing! We ordered a three-octave set of bells and, to our utter amazement, they arrived in three weeks. Both my husband and I were church musicians and public school music teachers; but neither of us had ever seen or heard a handbell choir, and none of the local bell choir directors offered us any help. We were on our own. Oh yes, the superintendent also said that he wanted this yet-to-be-organized bell choir to ring in church *soon*. Little did we know that, to him, soon meant *two or three weeks!* We had no choice about who would be in our first bell choir or what its purpose would be. The superintendent selected the children who would become ringers, and the new bell choir would join the singing choir on its weekly travels to lead Methodist congregations in worship each Sunday morning.

When we first began working with bells there were few sources to go to for help. Now there is much knowledgeable help available, and there are many different ways of developing good bell choir programs. We believe that directors should explore the possibilities, become well informed about the options, and choose what will best suit their needs. In the pages that follow, I hope to share with you some of the things that have worked for us in our handbell programs. These ideas are not *absolutes;* they are our *opinions*. Regard them as just that and use them if you think they will work for you.

"Handbell Helper"

Recipe for a Successful Handbell Choir

Ingredients
1 copy of *Handbell Helper*
750 to 2000 lbs. potential ringers
1 handbell director
handbells and assorted equipment
positive attitudes
regular attendance
leadership
patience
kindness
music elements
techniques
humor
fun
love
anticipation
discipline
favorite dressing or glaze

Preheat or precool rehearsal area to provide a ringer friendly atmosphere.

Add to 1 thoroughly studied copy of *Handbell Helper:* 750 to 2000 lbs. of potential ringers (8 to 13 ringers, both male and female) selected for their positive attitude and commitment to regular attendance.

Add 1 well-prepared director thoroughly saturated with leadership and patience.

Add handbells and equipment.

Sift out poor attitudes, laziness, and irresponsibility. Shape "loafs" into musically responsible ringers.

Chill any flaring tempers. Mix well with kindness.

Stir in all elements of music until mixture reaches desired consistency.

Blend techniques until fine.

Tenderize with a generous amount of love.

Sprinkle with a pinch of humor and a dash of fun.

Simmer with anticipation.

Saute with consistent, loving discipline.

Let marinate for two to three months, shaking and stirring at least forty-five minutes per week.

Arrange in uniform fashion and top with favorite dressing or glaze.

Do not underprepare.

The recipe may be doubled as many times as desired to satisfy growing appetites. After doubling, divide into as many performing portions as necessary.

Serves an unlimited number of ringers and listeners.

Happy Ringing!

Chapter One
Congratulations, You Are the New Handbell Director!

B efore you can begin your work as a new bell choir director or as a director who is beginning a new handbell program, you and your church (or sponsoring organization) must decide the purpose of the handbell program and who may participate. If the primary function of the bell choir is to provide music for worship services, you must carefully select music suitable for worship and train the ringers to be responsible worship leaders. If the main purpose of the choir is an educational one, you will want to teach your ringers to read music and also to teach them as much as possible about the music they are learning to ring. If performance is the main reason for being, you will want to spend most of the rehearsal time learning and perfecting music for worship or concert. Whatever the purpose of the choir, you must carefully plan your rehearsals to allow the group to achieve its goals.

After the purpose of the bell choir has been determined, you must address the question, "Who may participate in the handbell program or in a specific bell choir?" These additional questions will need answering:

♪ Must the ringers be good music readers or will the handbell program be open to anyone who will make the necessary commitment, regardless of music-reading abilities?

♪ What age-level choirs will be formed?

♪ How many choirs will be organized?

♪ How will ringers be recruited?

♪ Will there be tryouts?

There are no right or wrong answers to these questions. Each director must develop his or her own philosophy regarding the purpose of the bell program, determine the needs of the program, and decide what will work best under those circumstances. Let us review the questions again.

1. **"Who will be allowed to participate in the handbell program?"** In 1970, when my husband and I became the first ministers of music at St. James United Methodist Church in Little Rock, Arkansas, the church decided that the bell program would be open to any and all who wanted to ring and who would make the necessary commitment. It is a decision we have never regretted! Although the ability to read music is an asset, our ringers are not required to have that skill. We have developed a color-coding system that allows non-music-readers as well as musicians to fully participate in the bell choir. This system will be discussed in chapter 7.

2. **"What age-level choir(s) will be formed?"** We have a graded program that provides a ringing opportunity for everyone from fourth grader through adult, but many churches do not have this luxury. It is not important that you have a large, graded bell program, but rather that you have a program that meets the needs of your church. That may be only one bell choir! What are your human resources? What age groups have enough people interested in forming a bell choir? Do not neglect any age group. The youth will progress faster than any other age group, but a children's choir is needed as a feeder group for the youth choir. Adults are often forgotten, but they are anxious to ring, too. For many of them, this is their "therapy time," after a hard day's work! The senior adults should not be neglected, either.

3. **"How will ringers be recruited?"** An open invitation can be made through the church newsletter, the worship bulletin, by a music or special brochure, or by any means the church has to communicate with its membership. However, the most effective tool is personal contact. This can come during Sunday school time, at youth group meetings, or at the various choir rehearsals. A personal contact or invitation from another ringer or from you, the handbell director, is a powerful and effective recruitment tool. Some people are waiting for their own personal invitation!

4. **"Will there be tryouts?"** If you choose or need to have tryouts, make them nonexclusive. Use them as fact-finding, information-gathering times to learn where the ringers are musically. Find out if they can read music, or if they can identify musical symbols even if they are not good music readers. Devise non-musical games and activities that will check their coordination and their ability to follow verbal cues. Rather than use the information gathered to exclude people from the program, use it to place them in a group where they will be the most comfortable and to which they can make the greatest contribution.

Earlier in this chapter we asked you to develop your own philosophy about the purpose of your handbell program. To help you do that, let us share ours with you. We have chosen to make the handbell program a program of Christian outreach to the whole church, not just to the musically literate. It is a tool for witnessing to our congregation, to our community, and through our participation in regional and national handbell activities, a tool for witnessing throughout the country. It is a means of getting people involved in active church participation. It is a ministry through which they can serve their church, and for many it is a point of entry into the church. Time and time again we have seen people become involved in the music ministry and through that experience be led into Christian discipleship.

Long ago we discovered that there was much more to bell choir than just ringing a handbell. In addition to music, through the small-group, one-on-one experience, we try to teach or instill in the ringers:

♪ A love for the church
♪ An appreciation for good music
♪ Commitment to a group and to a task
♪ The importance of discipline and self-discipline
♪ The importance of accepting and fulfilling responsibility
♪ The value of teamwork
♪ The importance of giving one's best at all times

The job is a big one. It is not easy, but it is worth the time and effort when you see the positive effect that participation in a handbell choir can have on all those involved!

Chapter Two
Equipment

Several years ago a little girl asked me, "Mrs. Thompson, will you please teach me to play the piano?" For some unexplainable reason I asked, "Kristen, do you have a piano?" She did not, so our conversation quickly came to a halt. I wonder if you are like Kristen or if it is safe to assume that you, the reader, have a set of handbells with which to work. If not, I hope you soon will.

There are two major manufacturers of handbells in the United States and one in London, England. I would not presume to recommend one foundry over another, but will give the addresses and phone numbers of each so that you may contact them if you need to purchase a set of bells or add to an existing set.

Malmark, Inc.
P.O. Box 1200
Plumsteadville, PA 18949
1-800-HANDBEL (426-3235)

Schulmerich Carillons
P.O. Box 903
Sellersville, PA 18960-0903
1-800-423-7464

Whitechapel Bell Foundry, Ltd.
32 & 34 Whitechapel Road
London E1 1DY, England
24-hour phone: +44 171 247 8598
FAX: +44 171 375 1979

Before purchasing a new set of handbells, if you have not already selected the manufacturer from which to order your bells, contact churches in your area who have Malmark, Schulmerich, and Whitechapel bells. Visit with the handbell directors. Attend bell choir rehearsals. Ring the bells so that you can feel and hear the differences in the ones from each manufacturer. Then you can decide which you prefer. Perhaps you could even arrange to hear the different sets of bells in your own church/school location before making a selection.

Handbell sets are purchased by the octave, and the two-octave set is considered the smallest practical size for a bell choir to use. Three-, four-, five-, and six-octave sets are also available. If your resources, both human and financial, allow the purchase of a three-octave set, I would recommend purchasing three octaves rather than two. Although there is much good music available for two octaves of bells, there is much more available for three or more octaves. I would also recommend purchasing the manufacturer's cases to store and move the bells. This is the safest and best way to protect the bells when they are not being used or when they are being transported from one place to another.

The chart below will allow you to quickly see which bells are included in each size set. The staff above the keyboard shows the written pitch of each bell and the keyboard shows its letter name and octave number. Handbells sound an octave higher than the written pitch.

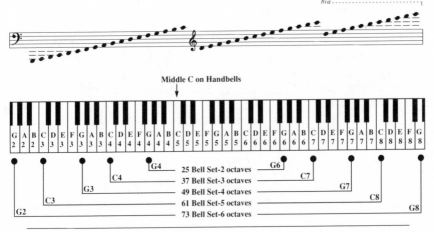

13

Care and Maintenance Items

The following care and maintenance items are included in the purchase of each new set of bells:

♪ A manual with care and maintenance information and diagrams
♪ Any special tools needed to make adjustments on the bells
♪ A polishing cloth
♪ A tube of handbell polish

Sometimes the manufacturers include instructional material and/or sample music for beginning bell choirs. There may also be a brochure of handbell accessories that may be purchased from the manufacturer and a list of resources for purchasing music and materials for the bell choir. If the bells you will be using were not purchased recently and you find that some of these items have been misplaced, additional ones may be ordered from the handbell manufacturer. Additional resource information may be obtained from the national office of the American Guild of English Handbell Ringers in Dayton, Ohio. (See chapter 16 for more information.)

Although one polishing cloth will be included with each set of new bells, you should purchase extra cloths so that each ringer will have one. After each rehearsal or performance, ringers should first use the inner cloth, treated with jeweler's rouge, to polish the bells and remove any fingerprints found on the castings. Then the bell should be buffed with the outer cloth. The bells should be thoroughly cleaned as often as necessary with nonabrasive handbell polish to remove smudges, fingerprints, and tarnish. Dry, clean, soft cloths (not the polishing cloths described above) should be used to apply the polishing cream and to remove it.

Tables

Before you can schedule the first bell choir rehearsal, you will need equipment and accessories in addition to the handbells. Tables are most important. They must be sturdy enough to support the bells, wide enough (thirty to thirty-six inches) to accommodate the bells and usually the music notebook, and high enough (twenty-nine to thirty-two inches) to allow the ringers to stand erect when changing bells. Both Malmark and Schulmerich, as well as independent handbell supply companies, sell tables made especially for bell choirs. Some tables are quite portable, others are not. Some have adjustable legs so that the table height can be changed. If portability is not a necessity, another option is to use the six-foot or eight-foot folding banquet tables owned by most churches and schools. Adjustable-height banquet tables are also available and are recommended if you choose to use this type of table. It is extremely important that the ringers have sufficient table space. A rule of thumb would be to allow a minimum of two feet per ringer. Intermediate and advanced ringers who are assigned numerous bells and those ringers who are assigned the very low bells may need additional table space.

Foam Table Pads

Some type of padding must be placed on top of the tables to protect the bells. Although blankets, quilts, or carpet squares could be used initially, foam pads are the best choice. Pads may be cut from sheets or rolls of upholstery foam, but the simplest and best thing to do is to purchase foam padding from Malmark or Schulmerich or from a handbell supply company. These pads are precut to fit three-foot or six-foot tables and are of a density suitable for handbell performance.

Foam handbell pads come in different thicknesses and densities. Regarding thickness, today most experts recommend four-inch padding for all but the smallest sets of bells. Regarding density, foam sold by handbell manufacturers and handbell supply companies comes in "super-soft" or "regular." The "super-soft" foam has a lot of air space in it and is quite flexible. The bells will sink into it, they will be easily damped (silenced), and they will not have a tendency to roll. However, when percussive techniques such as martellato or martellato lift (see chapter 9) are executed on "super-soft" foam, it may be too soft. It may allow the larger bells of the fifth and sixth octave (G2-F#3) and maybe even the low bells of the fourth octave (G3-B3) to press through the foam and strike the top of the table, causing damage to the bell casting. "Regular" density foam pads are firmer and provide better protection for the bells when percussive techniques are performed.

> **WARNING: Improper use of martellato and other percussive techniques may cause damage to the handbell casting.**

Table Coverings

Because of the chemicals found in the foam, the padding should be covered with some type of cloth. Each pad may be individually slipcovered, or tables and pads may be covered with a length of cloth, preferably cotton. In the rehearsal area, the following make good table covers:

♪ Twin bedspreads
♪ Fabric tablecloths (no plastic, please!)
♪ Twin sheets
♪ Lengths of cloth purchased from a fabric store

Table coverings for worship and performance should be selected for durability, practicality, portability, and appropriateness for the worship/concert setting. Many handbell experts recommend pinwale corduroy as the fabric of choice. You will probably want these covers to reach to the floor in front of the tables so the cases and equipment can be hidden beneath the tables when not in use during the service or concert. Special coverings may be tailored to meet your needs. Some directors prefer to have fitted coverings for each individual table. This makes a nice presentation, but the tables used must always be the same length and height or the coverings will not fit properly. Because we often play in different configurations and use differing lengths of table space, we have always chosen to use nonfitted, throw-style coverings. This usually means that, if lengths of fabric 45" to 60" wide are purchased, it will be necessary to have one and a half lengths of fabric in each table covering. One fabric that is an exception to this is felt. Although it is difficult to find, it is now possible to purchase a high-quality, washable felt that comes in a wide variety of colors. When using felt, one length of 72" fabric covers the tables from the floor in front, across the tabletop, and allows ample fabric to hang from the ringers' side of the table. When purchasing lengths of fabric for throw-style coverings, allow at least an eighteen-inch drop at the end of each table. An even longer drop is needed on the end tables if the covers are to reach the floor on the ends of the outer tables.

Music Notebooks and Stands

Today, three-ring notebooks that fold out into easel-type stands seem to be the most popular and practical method of holding and displaying music for the ringers. These come in a variety of sizes and colors, with notebook rings in various sizes. Other options are folding music stands that sit on the tables or choral/orchestral music stands that are placed on the floor in front of the tables. Bass ringers often prefer these floor stands because they do not take up valuable table space, which the large bells require. Music risers (usually made of metal, polyurethane, or wood) that are placed on the table to raise the easel notebooks eight to ten inches above the tabletop are becoming very popular. Music risers help all ringers see the director, and the risers may be especially helpful to those who wear bifocals and trifocals.

Gloves

Wearing gloves while handling and ringing bells is standard practice for today's ringers. (However, this has not always been so, and there are still some bell choirs who choose not to wear gloves while ringing.) Gloves keep the bell casting from tarnishing when it is touched by ringers' hands. Gloves also cushion and protect the ringers' hands during rehearsals and performances.

We have always found it advantageous to have separate sets of gloves for performance and rehearsal. Most groups wear white cotton gloves for performance, but some choose other colors (usually black). These can be purchased from handbell manufacturers, handbell supply stores, military supply stores, or from companies that manufacture band uniforms. There are even special handbell gloves that have gripper-dots in the palms to prevent the bells from slipping in the ringers' hands.

For rehearsal, we have always preferred cloth garden gloves purchased from the local home improvement or garden store. These come in several sizes and styles, and because they are made of a thicker fabric than the white cotton performance gloves, they do a better job of protecting the ringers' hands during long rehearsal sessions.

We purchase gloves by the dozen and supply them for all our ringers. We buy cloth garden gloves in several sizes and colors for rehearsal and white cotton gloves in various sizes for worship and performance. Some directors require ringers to purchase their own practice and performance gloves. In either case, the gloves can be kept with the bell equipment yet they can be identified and stored so that each ringer always wears his or her own gloves. You will have to weigh the pros and cons and decide what is best for your situation.

Mallets

Sooner or later you will want and need to invest in mallets for your ringers. More and more of today's handbell music incorporates techniques that require the use of mallets. Both Malmark and Schulmerich make special handbell mallets, as do some handbell supply stores. These mallets come in varying degrees of hardness or density, and they may be purchased in sets that include one mallet of each hardness and density. I would recommend buying one or two sets of mallets until, from experience, you determine that you need to purchase additional mallets of a specific hardness and density.

As a general rule, the lower the bell, the softer the mallet; the higher the bell, the firmer the mallet. It is extremely important that the proper density mallet be used on each bell, otherwise the bell may be damaged. Mallets made especially for use on hand-bells usually have written on the handle a designation of the range of bells for which they are particularly suited. To determine the proper mallet to use on each bell, follow this rule: When used to strike a bell on the outside of the casting near the lip of the bell (at approximately the same place as the clapper strikes the inside of the bell), a mallet should produce approximately the same sound as the clapper, on the soft setting, when it strikes the inside of the bell.

Lights

Small, high-intensity lights that can be clipped onto each note-book or music stand can be very helpful when the lighting in the worship service or performance area is too dim to allow ringers to see their music clearly. Handbell supply stores, and even some mail-order catalogues, have battery-operated lights that might be useful to your ringers. Investigate the choices (and the need) before investing in any lights for your choir.

Storage Containers

From a practical standpoint, you will need some way to store mallets, rehearsal gloves, performance gloves, and other equip-ment you will eventually accumulate. You can invest in storage containers that are designed for specific types of handbell equip-ment, or you can look around the church or house and find some-thing that works equally well. If you choose not to purchase con-tainers made especially for mallets, gloves, and so on, here are some alternate types of storage containers:

Mallets: Sturdy cardboard shipping boxes, especially those used to ship fruit

Rehearsal Gloves: (When provided by the organization and
washed after each use)
♪ Large multigallon cans that are used to store and ship
popped corn
♪ Plastic crates similar to milk carton crates
(You might want two containers, one for left-hand gloves,
one for right-hand gloves.)
Performance Gloves: (When provided by the organization and
washed after each performance)
♪ Net, zippered laundry bags; each bag labeled with the glove
size
♪ Gloves can be washed and dried in these bags, too! It will
save sorting time.
Rehearsal and Performance Gloves: (When owned by ringers and
not shared)
♪ Plastic bags with zip-top closure
♪ Zippered plastic pencil holders that fit into notebook binders

Carts and Dollies

Carts and dollies are wonderful when bells and equipment have
to be moved from rehearsal space to worship/performance space!
There are many styles and kinds of wheeled carts on the market,
so it is important that you purchase those that will accommodate
the bell cases and equipment you need to move. It is also important that the carts be sturdy enough to support the weight you
intend to put on them. Handbell equipment is not lightweight, so
unless you buy carts that will support at least two hundred
pounds, you will be making multiple trips to move all the equipment. Make certain that the bed of the cart is long enough to hold
the longest bell case. If you do not go to the extreme, other bell
cases and equipment may be stacked on top of the largest case. If
you plan to move modular tables on carts, you will probably need
a cart that is designed to move at least four hundred pounds of
equipment. You can also buy dollies that roll on four wheels or
that can be converted into two-wheeled dollies. The handle can
be fitted into the cart bed at a right angle to make a four-wheeled

cart or it can be inserted into the end of the cart bed to convert it into a two-wheeled dolly.

A WORD TO THE WISE: Be sure that the doors through which you must move your carts and equipment are wide enough for you to wheel the equipment through them!

When we move our modular tables, we must load them onto the cart outside the rehearsal room because the door to that room is not as wide as the tables!

Factors to Consider When Purchasing Carts and Dollies
Strength: Will it support the weight you need to put on it?
Portability: Does it fold/collapse to fit into a car trunk or van?
Weight: Is it light enough that it can be lifted into a car trunk or van?
Wheel size: Are the wheels large enough to allow the cart to roll easily? Carts that will be used to carry heavy loads should have relatively large wheels for easy movement.

For limited use in moving bell cases, we have found it possible to attach a pull-rope to a wheeled platform much like a skateboard. Some of these are homemade; one was purchased from a garden supply store. They are not fancy, but they do the job.

The Rehearsal Room

I have spent many hours in a far-too-small rehearsal room (heated by children's body heat!), so I know the importance of adequate rehearsal space, adequate ventilation, and good lighting! If possible, the ceiling of the rehearsal room should be higher than that of the average classroom, and the space should be large enough for the bell tables to be set up in the desired configuration. We prefer to have our tables in a U-shape so that the ringers can both see and hear one another. If a U-shape is not possible, our next choice would be an L-shape. Ringers in bell choirs that must ring in a straight line often have difficulty hearing one another. Using the two-feet-per-ringer rule of thumb, a three-octave bell choir would need twenty-two to twenty-four feet of table space. Choirs using larger bell sets would need more table space, perhaps between thirty and thirty-six feet. These groups may have a very difficult time ringing in a straight line.

Often rehearsal space must be shared with other groups such as vocal choirs and Sunday school classes. Sometimes handbell choirs must rehearse in the sanctuary. If these conditions are initially viewed as disadvantages, why not see if they also have advantages for you? In a choir room or sanctuary you would probably have a piano or organ at your disposal. This can be helpful when working with beginning choirs, and it can be a big advantage when learning music for bells and keyboard. Those choirs that must always rehearse in the sanctuary will be accustomed to ringing in that space when they ring for worship. Few of us have the luxury of a spacious room designed especially for handbell rehearsals (fortunately we do!), so look for ways to make the best use of the space available. Turn your minuses into pluses!

Chapter Three
Selecting Music

Poor music performed well is still poor music! Before we look at factors to consider in selecting music for the *beginning* bell choir, let us look at some criteria for selecting music for *any* bell choir.

Criteria for Selecting All Handbell Music

- ♪ Musically sound
- ♪ Suitable for handbells
- ♪ Sounds good on handbells
- ♪ Well written in the handbell idiom
- ♪ Uses enough bells consistently to keep the ringers busy
- ♪ Is age-appropriate, level-appropriate, and of interest to the ringers

Musically Sound: Musical tastes and styles differ, but the elements that make up a musically sound composition should be evident in all the music chosen for your bell choirs. Each piece should have good form; a sense of direction; melodic, rhythmic, and harmonic interest; and should not be trite in any sense of the word. As you begin purchasing music for your bell choir, remember that you are building a library for use now and in the years to come. Select music that will stand the test of time and buy wisely.

Suitable for Handbells/Sounds Good on Handbells/Well written in the Handbell Idiom: It is difficult to separate these three criteria. Music that is well written for handbells should sound better on bells than it does on the piano or on any other instrument. If it is well written in the handbell idiom, it will make the bells seem to do things that some would not think possible. It will utilize the brilliance yet fast-fading qualities of the high bells while taking advantage of the round sonorities of the large bass bells. It will employ rhythms to create interest and movement. It may incorporate various handbell techniques in addition to the usual, straight-ringing technique. It will be well crafted by a composer/arranger who has worked with handbells and is familiar with their strengths and weaknesses.

Uses Enough Bells Consistently to Keep Ringers Busy: Do not be tempted to determine this solely by the number of bells used (the number of bells listed in the handbells used chart). Sometimes these charts list many bells, but you may find that certain ones are not used very often. Study the music to see if all of the ringers will have enough to do. After reading chapter 5, you will be better able to make this assessment. Idle ringers (especially children and beginners) can cause problems when they are not busy. If they are not busy ringing, they will be busy distracting other ringers and you!

Is Age-appropriate, Level-appropriate, and of Interest to the Ringers: Music that interests adults may not interest children, but adults may not mind learning to ring by using the same music you use for the children. Youth ringers want music that speaks to them—music that is rhythmically interesting. Given a choice, most youth would opt for "fast and loud," but they need to learn that not everything can be fast and loud! They need to develop the discipline required to ring beautiful melodies and to ring "soft and slow" sections and selections that provide contrast in their repertoire. Teenagers do not realize that this is far more difficult than ringing everything at breakneck speed!

Our youth are especially fond of ringing arrangements and transcriptions of the classics. This exposes them to great music that has stood the test of time, and it gives them an appreciation for music they might not otherwise know. Television cartoons and advertisements often use excerpts from the classics as background music. Take advantage of this and use some of these themes with bell choirs. You can even find arrangements that have been written especially for beginners. Tailor the selection of music to fit each bell choir. Select music that interests them, that speaks to their age group, that encourages them to grow musically, and that helps them develop good musical tastes.

Selecting Music for the Beginning Bell Choir

Full Chords: *The most disastrous thing you can ask a beginning bell choir to do is to ring a single-line melody!* If one ringer gets lost, everything can fall apart or come to a screeching halt! Full chords give the ringers security. Beginning ringers of all ages will at some time get lost. When they do, the full chords will provide a good cover-up for them. One or two notes missing from an eight-to-twelve-note chord is not very noticeable.

Long Note Values: For the very first pieces you use with beginners, look for music that has mostly whole notes and half notes. Beginners need to concentrate on many things, so after ringing a note, they need a long time to think about what to do next. Whole notes give them a chance to do that. After ringing the first note, they have three beats to get ready to ring the second note.

Simple Rhythms: After learning to ring whole-note chords, half-note and quarter-note chords may be gradually introduced. These are more difficult for beginners because they require a quicker response than ringing whole notes. There is not as much time to prepare between notes. Keep the rhythms steady and simple and use quarter notes sparingly at first.

Few, If Any, Eighth Notes: You must get your ringers ringing *on* the beats before trying to get them to ring *between* the beats. No matter what you do, some of them will be ringing between the beats anyway! Save the eighth notes until later.

Slow Harmonic Changes: Slow harmonic changes require less damping. (To damp a bell is to stop it from ringing, to silence it.) Damping is difficult for beginners. They are so busy thinking about *ringing* that they have little time to think about *damping* their bells. If the harmony remains constant for several beats (or even for a measure or two) ringers can concentrate on ringing and not on having to damp their bells after one beat.

Selecting music with slow-moving harmony will allow the choir to ring successfully music that sounds much more difficult than it really is.

Few (or No) Chromatics: Chromatics usually require ringers to put down one bell and pick up another. Ringers need time to become accustomed to ringing one or two bells throughout an entire piece of music before they are asked to make any bell changes. Wait awhile before introducing chromatics.

Comfortable Meter: Common time (4/4) is the best meter for beginners, at least for American beginners! We are far more accustomed to hearing marches and music in 4/4 time than we are to hearing waltzes and music in 3/4 time. If we had grown up in Vienna this might not be the case! Have your ringers feel comfortable ringing music in 4/4 time before you introduce the 3/4 meter. Avoid 6/8 until the choir has progressed well beyond the beginner stage.

Techniques: The first pieces chosen should require only the usual straight ringing technique. The basic ringing stroke has to be mastered before any special techniques are introduced. The easiest way to introduce a new technique is to have everyone learn it at the same time—everyone learns to pluck, thumb damp, swing, or shake. Then have everyone play a section or an entire piece of music using the newly learned technique. It is easier and more effective to teach this way than it is to combine techniques and ask some to ring and some to learn the new technique.

Familiar Melodies: Ringers enjoy playing melodies they already know. If you choose arrangements of tunes that are already familiar to them, they can more quickly tell whether or not they have rung the music correctly.

Moderate Tempo: Select music that does not have to be played *vivace* to sound right. This does not mean that the music cannot be exciting, but it does mean that when it is learned, a moderate tempo will be appropriate.

No Page Turns: Page turning is an "advanced technique." Page turns are difficult for anyone wearing gloves, and they are particularly difficult for beginners. Be conscious of this as you select music for your choir.

There Should Be Enough Happening Musically to Keep the Ringers Actively Involved and Busy: Beginners tend to get lost when they ring only occasionally. Music that lets them ring steadily and consistently helps keep them from getting lost, it keeps them from being bored, and it keeps them out of trouble. A ringer who has little or nothing to ring will find ways to keep busy, and ways to annoy you and the other ringers!

Use of a Keyboard Instrument: The addition of a keyboard accompaniment to a beginning bell piece can make the choir sound big and important. This is similar to the concept of having a beginning piano student play duets with the teacher. The student's ego is boosted and he or she sounds great even though the teacher is the one doing all the hard work. The same principle can apply to music arranged for bell choir and keyboard. The bell choir usually rings a rather simple part while the accompanist does the more difficult work. An accompanist who really watches and follows the director can also be a steadying force, helping to keep the tempo consistent and the ringers together. Beginners have a difficult time following a director, even if or when they remember to look up!

Finding Music that Meets These Criteria

In the early 1980s, when we were unable to find printed music that would meet the needs of our beginning bell choirs, Fran Callahan and I decided to write our own arrangements. We used the criteria listed above as guidelines for our writing. What began as a project for our own use resulted in four series of books for the beginning bell choir. The books in the *Ready to Ring, Begin to Ring, Time to Ring,* and *Clapper Classics* series each begin with music that can be used at a bell choir's first rehearsal. Always adhering to the adopted criteria, the arrangements allow the ringers to grow musically and to increase their ringing skills as they progress through any of the collections. (The titles of the thirteen books in these series may be found in chapter 16.)

Music and the Copyright Law

Copying Music Is Illegal! It's as simple as that! Anything that is protected by copyright, that bears the copyright symbol ©, can legally be copied only by the copyright owner. Purchase enough copies for you and your ringers. (The minimum number of copies of music needed would be one for every two ringers and one for the director. For various reasons, you may want to buy a copy of music for each ringer.) Don't be tempted to use the copy machine rather than purchasing the music.

Copying Music Is Stealing! If you ran out of grape juice at a communion service you would not think of going to the grocery store and stealing some! When we copy music (or any copyrighted material) we are stealing from composers, arrangers, and publishers who depend on music sales for their income.

Churches Should Set the Right Kind of Example. Obey the law because it is the right thing to do. There are also substantial fines for those caught disregarding the law!

Chapter Four
Bell Distribution Systems

What Am I Going to Do with All the Bells?

Years ago, before it was customary for churches to have computer systems, several staff members and I went to "computer school" to learn the basics of using the system our church had installed. At that time, our big dream was to have the computer print mailing labels! After we had listened to the instructor drone on for about eight hours without our understanding much of what he had said (mailing labels were never even mentioned!), he turned to us and asked, "Does anyone have any questions?" The church secretary shyly raised her hand and asked, "How do you turn it on?"

Deciding how to distribute all those bells among the ringers is just as important as learning how to turn on the computer! Because beginning directors need a starting place, this chapter will explain:

♪ The standard method of assigning two octaves of bells
♪ The standard method of assigning three octaves of bells
♪ The standard methods of assigning four and five octaves of bells
♪ Some nonstandard or unusual ways of assigning bells
♪ The way we assign our bells for three or more octaves

Before describing the standard ways of assigning bells for the various size bell sets, I want to share some general thoughts about assignment methods.

♪ There is no right or wrong way to assign bells as long as all bells are assigned and the assignments work. (See the final paragraph of this chapter.)
♪ We must respect others' methods of assigning bells.
♪ We should be open-minded and learn from one another.

After studying this chapter, you should decide which assignment system you want to try with your choirs. Although you may eventually want to change your mind, try another system, or develop one of your own, until you have more experience in assigning bells, I would suggest you start with one of the distribution systems outlined here. Whatever you do, keep these three things in mind:

♪ Have a method.
♪ Know why you are doing what you are doing.
♪ Be consistent in everything you do.

Standard Assignments for Two Octaves

Ringer	Bells
#1	G4, A4
#2	B4, C5
#3	D5, E5
#4	F5, G5
#5	A5, B5
#6	C6, D6
#7	E6, F6
#8	G6

Normally seven or eight ringers are used to cover two octaves of bells. Each ringer has two diatonic notes (C and D, E and F, G and A, or B and C; these are bells without sharps or flats on their handles). If there are only seven ringers, the G6 is assigned to whichever ringer can handle it in addition to his or her regularly assigned bells. If there are eight ringers, the eighth ringer has only the G6.

Although it is not specifically indicated, ringers share the chromatics. That means that, at position #1, if a note were written as A-sharp, ringer #1 would usually be responsible for ringing it. If the note were written as B-flat, it would become ringer #2's responsibility. Of course there are exceptions to this assumption, and there may be times when this sharing will be unnecessary or impossible.

If your choir will soon be ringing three or more octaves of bells, to save confusion, you might want to begin your two-octave assignments at position #3, leaving positions #1 and #2 vacant. If you do this, the position numbers can remain the same no matter how many octaves of bells are rung. (See the next paragraph.)

Standard Assignments for Three Octaves

Ringer	Bells
#1	C4, D4
#2	E4, F4
#3	G4, A4
#4	B4, C5
#5	D5, E5
#6	F5, G5
#7	A5, B5
#8	C6, D6
#9	E6, F6
#10	G6, A6
#11	B6, C7

Using this system, eleven ringers are needed to cover the three-octave range. Although it requires more ringers to cover the three-octave range, this distribution has the following elements in common with the two-octave distribution:

♪ Ringers share the chromatics.

♪ Each ringer has two diatonic notes (see illustration above).

♪ Each ringer has a space note in the left hand and a line note in the right hand.

Assigning Four and Five Octaves of Bells

As you have probably discovered, when you purchase an additional octave of bells, you are buying both high and low bells, bells above and below the set of bells you already have. (See chapter 2 for the ranges of the different size bell sets.) When assigning bells for the four- and five-octave ranges, many directors who use the standard distribution system for the three-octave bell set handle the assignment of the additional bells in this way:

♪ The bells below C4 and above C7 become **floater** bells.

♪ These **floater** bells are assigned, composition to composition, to the ringers who can best handle them in addition to the bells regularly assigned to their ringing positions.

♪ The **bass floater** bells are assigned first (those from C3 to B3) because their size and weight makes them difficult to handle.

♪ The **treble floater** bells are assigned next. They are somewhat
   easier to assign than the large bass floater bells.

Some directors add one or two ringers to help handle these larger
sets of bells. In all but our beginning bell choirs, we use thirteen
ringers because we normally ring music written for four or five
octaves of bells. Usually the additional ringers are added in the
bass bell range. The fourth- and fifth-octave bass bells may be
divided in one or more of the following ways:

♪ One ringer is assigned the busiest of the following combina-
   tions of bells: G3 and A3, or A3 and B3, or G3 and B3.

♪ A second, additional ringer helps cover the remaining low
   bells.

♪ The remaining low bells are assigned (by the director) where
   they can be handled best.

♪ The assignment of these bells varies from one piece of music
   to another.

When assigning bells above C7, some directors using the standard
distribution system will assign the bells wherever they can be handled in the most musical way. Preference is usually given to those
ringers who are least busy and need more to ring. (This is how we
prefer to assign these bells.) Other directors will assign the bells
of the upper octave to those ringers who have the same pitches an
octave lower:

♪ D7 is assigned to the D6 ringer.

♪ E7 and F7 are assigned to the E6 and F6 ringer.

♪ G7 and A7 are assigned to the G6 and A6 ringer.

♪ B7 and C8 are assigned to the B6 and C7 ringer.

For those who use this second method, the assumption is that
these bells can be Shelly rung in octaves. (See chapter 9 for a
description of Shelly ringing.) In theory this would solve all
assignment problems, but in reality we have found that, more
often than not, this distribution of high bells will not work for us.
When it does work, it is most often with the G7 to C8 bells. Problems often arise with the D7 to F7 bells because, in this range,
often one of the two bells is to be rung on a given beat (and the
other is not), or the two bells are to be rung using two different
techniques. One may be rung, the other shaken; one may be rung,

the other martellato; one may be rung, the other thumb-damped, and so on. (See chapter 9 for a description of these techniques.)

Nontraditional Bell Distribution Systems

As we said at the beginning of this chapter, there is no right or wrong way to assign bells as long as all bells are assigned and the assignment system works for the person using it. Many directors do use the bell distribution systems outlined above, but we must not assume that all directors do.

Some distribution systems intentionally break the two-diatonics-per-ringer grouping. This break can come at any place, but often it happens at the position that normally would be assigned A5 and B5. Now this ringer is assigned only A5. (In addition to A5, this position will be assigned one or more floater bells.) The next position then has B5 and C6, and two-diatonics-per-ringer is resumed from that point upward. Therefore, it is not safe to assume that, in all systems, one ringer will be assigned A5 and B5, one assigned C6 and D6, or that B6 and C7 will be in the hands of the same ringer.

At this point, describing some of the other nontraditional ways of assigning bells would probably confuse the issue. Right now all you need to know is that these systems exist, that they are all valid, and that they are being used successfully by outstanding choirs.

Our Bell Distribution System

Before I describe our distribution system (which really isn't so unusual), I want to explain how and why this system came about. When we began working with handbells in 1966, we received no help from any directors in our area. We were completely on our own! We had a new three-octave set of bells and a book that was included in the bell shipment. This book said that if we had two octaves of bells, we needed "X" number of ringers and the bells should be assigned in such-and-such a way. If we had three octaves of bells, we needed "X" number of ringers and the bells should be assigned in a slightly different way. We had three octaves of bells. The book said we needed fewer than twelve ringers, but our boss, the superintendent of the Methodist Children's Home, said that we would have twelve ringers in the bell choir. Not knowing any better, we arbitrarily divided one or two of the assignment positions listed in the book, and what we did worked!

When we expanded our three-octave set of bells, we kept the same basic distribution system we had devised, and it still worked! By that time, handbell music was becoming more difficult and complex, though it was still very simple by today's standards. We were also gaining experience and expertise in making bell assignments. We simply adapted our system to accommodate the four- and five-octave bell sets. Here is the bell distribution we have used since 1966. The first is for two octaves of bells, the second for three octaves.

Thompson Method of Assigning Two Octaves

Ringer	Bells
#3	G4, G#/Ab4
#4	A4, A#/Bb4
#5	B4, C5
#6	C#/Db5, D5, D#/Eb5
#7	E5, F5
#8	F#/Gb5, G5
#9	G#/Ab5, A5, A#/Bb5
#10	B5, C6, C#/Db6
#11	D6, D#/Eb6, E6
#12	F6, F#/Gb6, G6

Since we have enough ringers to ring three octaves of bells with all our groups, we rarely ring two-octave music. However, when we do, we divide the bells in one of two ways, depending on whether we need to have parts for nine or for ten ringers. The division above is what we use for ten ringers. When we use only nine ringers, we combine positions #3 and #4, placing the bells at position #4. Ringers #4 and #5 then share the responsibility for the A#/Bb4. All other assignments remain the same.

Thompson Method of Assigning Three Octaves

(Ringers share bells in parentheses.)

Ringer	Bells
#1	C4, C#/Db4, D4, (D#4
#2	Eb4), E4, F4, (F#4
#3	Gb4), G4, G#/Ab4
#4	A4, A#/Bb4
#5	B4, C5
#6	C#/Db5, D5, D#/Eb5
#7	E5, F5
#8	F#/Gb5, G5
#9	G#/Ab5, A5, A#/Bb5
#10	B5, C6, C#/Db6
#11	D6, D#/Eb6, E6
#12	F6, F#/Gbb6, G6

If we combine more positions, we can ring two-octave music with fewer than nine ringers. Later in this chapter we describe additional ways to combine positions. By always beginning our two-octave assignments at positions #3 or #4, without changing our basic assignment or table setup, we can easily add the bottom positions (#1, #2, and sometimes #3) when we ring three-octave music.

As you can see, our basic assignments are for slightly less than three octaves. They start at the bottom of the third octave (C4) and end at the top of the second octave (G6). This means that, in three-octave music, G#6 through C7 are floater bells. Often, especially in beginning music, these bells are not used enough in a given piece of music to keep a ringer busy if A6 and B6 or B6 and C7 are assigned to one ringer. We prefer to assign these bells to the ringers who can handle them in the most musical way or to the ringers who are not busy enough and need to be more involved. If a ringer has nothing to do on the last page, he or she will lose interest and often cause discipline problems. By assigning that ringer a floater bell, usually he or she can be kept busy (and out of mischief) until the end of the piece of music. Also, having a mixture of bells (floater bells in addition to regularly assigned bells) can often make a given assignment more interesting and sometimes more challenging. Not being locked into a basic assignment pattern of two diatonic notes per ringer makes it much easier for us to assign music that is chromatic or that makes frequent use of accidentals.

Because we begin the range for our floater bells at a slightly lower point than is found in the standard distribution system, when we ring three-octave music, we always have floater bells to assign. Even with our beginning children's choirs we use three octaves of bells and this system works very well for them, too.

When we assign music for four and five octaves, we have more floater bells to assign because we now have both low and high bells that lie outside the range of our basic assignments. Once we advance beyond music for the beginning bell choir, we find that all the bells within the three-octave range are used consistently and ringers would be kept busy if assigned only bells in the G#6 to C7 range. We keep our basic assignments as the starting point, but we may find that we need to do some shifting within these basic assignments so that we can free entire positions to handle the floater bells. This is especially true in more difficult music and in music making full use of the entire five-octave range. We don't hesitate to shift bells from their normal positions if it is needed or if it is wise to do so. As we have said before, it is important to keep all ringers busy, involved, and challenged! In chapter 6 we will discuss criteria for deciding where to assign floater bells.

In the chart following you can see how we often shift bells and modify our basic distribution system when we assign music for the larger four- and five-octave bell sets.

You can see from this chart that we have added a "0" position. It is placed below position #1 and it is primarily used to handle the fourth- and/or fifth-octave low bells. Because music of this scope will usually be more complicated and difficult and there will be many more bells to assign, the extra ringer is very helpful. This can be a "catch-all" position, but it does not have to be. Our first strategy is to assign the busiest of the bass bells, especially the fifth-octave ones, here. This ringer can also have a mixture of high and low bells, or he or she can help handle the difficult-to-assign bells that cannot be rung at their normal positions. It is important that this position be justified and that the ringer be kept busy.

If you are fortunate enough to have five octaves of bells, it is important that you take great care in assigning the low bells (C3 to F#3). All of these bells are heavy! Depending on the manufacturer of the bell set, C3 can weigh between ten and thirteen pounds. Unless I know that there will be a ringer who can lift and ring these big bells with one hand (and then put them down using only one hand), I prefer to assign any bell E3 and below to a position where the ringer will have time to ring it with two hands. If power is needed, I always try to assign a very low bell where it can be rung with two hands.

Modifications to the Thompson Basic Bell Assignments (Four or More Octaves)

(Ringers may share bells in parentheses.)

Ringer	Bells
#0	No assigned bells
#1	C4, C#/Db4, D4, (D#4
#2	Eb4), E4, F4, (F#4
#3	May now be assigned low bells, high bells, or a mixture.
#4	Gb4), G4, G#/Ab4, A4, (A#4
#5	Bb4), B4, C5, (C#5
#6	Db5), D5, D#/Eb5, E5
#7	May now be assigned low bells, high bells, or a mixture
#8	F5, F#/Gb5, G5, (G#5
#9	Ab5), A5, (A#5
	May often have one hand free and can be assigned one or more floater bells.
#10	Bb5), B5, C6, (C#6
#11	Db6), D6, D3/Eb6, E6
#12	F6, F#/Gb6, G6

Not all age groups will be ringing the fifth-octave low bells. Children will seldom ring them, although there are ways to do so without really having to lift the bells. Women usually have difficulty lifting the low bells, and ringing them with one hand is impossible for some. Some junior high school boys and most senior high school boys can ring the biggest bells with one hand (so can some of the girls), but the assignment of these bells needs to be made with great thought and care.

I believe that the director should make the bell assignments prior to presenting the music to the choir. The director should know better than anyone the complexities of the music and the best way to distribute the bells for that piece. Assigning all bells before presenting the music to the bell choir also saves valuable rehearsal time. Personally, I want to address and solve problems before they happen. Sometimes a ringer is busy, sometimes not, but it all evens out in the long run. No ringer should be allowed to become a bell hog! The director should reassign any bell that could cause a ringer problems before that ringer "lays claim" to it. Although we try to teach them that the Christian way is to share, ringers are reluctant to give up "their" bells.

Thoughts About Bell Assignments

♪ An assignment problem may be solved by adding another ringer, but that may be a problem in itself.

♪ Good bell assignments facilitate accurate ringing and damping.

♪ Good bell assignments should meet all these criteria:
   ♪ They are feasible.
   ♪ They are possible.
   ♪ They are practical.
   ♪ They are logical.

♪ I do not know of a foolproof system that will work for every piece of music! I wish I did!

Chapter Five
Assigning Bells

Once you have decided which bell distribution system to use, you can begin the actual assigning process for your first piece of music. This always requires thought and careful planning, but as you gain experience you will find that the process becomes easier and the work goes faster. We all have a common goal—to assign all bells in such a way that the composition can be rung correctly and musically.

The ideas shared in this chapter have come from many hours (no, many years) of assigning bells. These ideas will work, regardless of the bell distribution system you use. My hope is that I can give you:

♪ A starting place
♪ A way to think through the assigning process
♪ A method for clearly putting your assignments and instructions on the music
♪ Tips that will help the ringers handle the logistics of ringing

I always begin the assigning process at the position that has the lowest of the regularly assigned bells, the position below which all bells are considered floater bells. Regardless of the distribution system used, this usually will be position #1. (When assigning two-octave music, for us this would be position #3.) As you study the music and carefully think through the first ringer's assignments, mentally or on paper, note the places where he or she cannot handle all the bells assigned to that position. In the back of your mind, begin planning where to place these difficult-to-assign bells. Repeat this process for all positions, noting places where a ringer cannot handle all his or her bells, possible places to assign these bells, and positions where ringers need more to do and could be assigned floater bells.

Let's think through position #1 in more detail. For illustration purposes, assume that the piece of music to be assigned is in the key of C and that ringer #1 will be responsible for C4 and D4. She will also be responsible for C#/D♭4 and D#4. If D#4 is written as E♭4, it will become the responsibility of ringer #2. First assign the C4 to be rung in the ringer's left hand. If there are any C#4's in the music, see if this bell can be exchanged consistently with the C4 and rung with the left hand. If so, that is good because this is a simple and logical bell change. Next assign the D4 to be rung in the ringer's right hand. If there are any D#4's in the music, see if this bell can be exchanged consistently with the D4 and rung with the right hand. If not, can it be exchanged consistently with the C4 and C#4? Although it would be nice to keep all the C's in the left hand and all the D's in the right hand, if the D#4's could always be rung with the left hand or the C#4's could always be rung with the right hand, go ahead and make the assignment. It is simple, it is consistent, and it is logical. If either C#4 or D#4 would consistently need to be rung with one hand and then the other, I would try to place this bell elsewhere if I were assigning music for beginning ringers. If I were assigning advanced music, I would not hesitate to make this type of assignment because the ringer would be expected to have the ringing experience and skill to handle it.

After assigning all ringer #1's bells, determine if there are any floater bells that she can easily and logically ring in addition to the bells already assigned to position #1. I do not actually assign the floater bells at this time, but I make a written note of the possibilities. I find that I can be most efficient if I do this now when I am familiar with what is happening in this position's assignment. If I wait until I have completed assigning all the positions, I have to refamiliarize myself with each position before I can see the possibilities for assigning floater bells. Later, when I see what is happening in all the other parts, I can decide which floater bells could best be handled by each ringer.

Determining which floater bells could be assigned to ringer #1 is important, but telling you how to do this is difficult. Let me illustrate with a simple example.

In this example the five bells that lie outside the three-octave range are:

Low bells: G3

High bells: D7, E7, F7, and G7

We will assume that you are using the standard distribution system and that all five bells are floater bells that you must assign. First, we should go back to ringer #1 and see if she can ring any of these floater bells in addition to the C4 and D4 that are already assigned to position #1.

♪ Can she ring the low G3? No, because the C4, rung with her left hand, must sound from count 1 until count 2. At that point she must ring D4 with her right hand. Since G3 must also be rung on count 3, there is no way ringer #1 could do this without cheating the value of the C4, which was rung on count 1. If she did ring the G3, she would have to cheat its value to pick up and ring the C4 in measure 2. In this example, ringer #1 should not be assigned the G3.

♪ Can she ring any of the four high bells? No, because she would have to cheat the values of the C4 or D4 to be able to ring any of the high bells since they all fall very close to counts 1 and 3. A quick-change artist might be able to ring the E7 or F7, but I would not make such an assignment, especially for beginning ringers.

At this point, having given ringer #1 all the bells normally assigned to that position and having determined (and noted) that she should not be assigned any of the floater bells, I would move on to position #2. I would follow this same process for assigning all the remaining ringing positions.

(If I had used the Thompson distribution system, there would have been twelve ringers instead of eleven, seven floater bells instead of five [B6 and C7 would have been added], there would have been eight "free hands" at seven positions to handle the floater bells, and no ringer would have been assigned more than two bells.)

To help me see the possibilities for placing floater bells, I have developed a graph on which I enter data after assigning the basic bells for each position. The more floater bells there are, the more helpful this information becomes. Using the two-measure example above as our "piece of music," the graph below illustrates the way I would enter information regarding each position's assignments:

♪ An "X" indicates that the ringer could not ring the floater bell.
♪ An "O" indicates that the ringer could ring the floater bell.
♪ A "?" means just that—probably not, but think about it.

Distribution Graph for Assigning Floater Bells

Ringer No.	Assigned Bells	Floaters: G3	D7	E7	F7	G7
#1	C4, D4	X	X	X	X	X
#2	E4, F4	O	O	O	O	O
#3	G4, A4	O	O	O	O	O
#4	B4, C5	X	X	X	X	X
#5	D5, E5	X	X	X	X	X
#6	F5, G5	X	X	X	X	X
#7	A5, B5	O	O	O	O	O
#8	C6, D6	X	X	X	X	X
#9	E6, F6	X	X	X	X	X
#10	G6, A6	O	O	O	O	O
#11	B6, C7	X	X	X	?	O

Using the information in this graph, I am now ready to start assigning the floater bells. There are five bells that need to be placed, and coincidentally there are five ringers who could handle one or more of them. In this case, it is a rather simple process of elimination, so this is how I would proceed:

♪ Ringer #11 could ring only the G7, so I would assign it there.
♪ The other four ringers could ring any of the remaining bells.
♪ Assign ringer #2 the G3 since this is the lowest floater bell and I would like to keep it in the bass bell range.
♪ In this example assigning the remaining high bells is arbitrary, so I would choose to assign the lowest remaining floater bell to the lowest position available, continuing upward through both position numbers and pitch of the floater bells.
♪ Assign ringer #3 the D7.
♪ Assign ringer #7 the E7.
♪ Assign ringer #10 the F7.

If you look at the rhythmic ringing patterns created for the ringers being assigned the high floater bells, you will see that each one is relatively simple. No ringer must ring an isolated eighth note. Anytime a ringer is assigned one of the notes falling between the beats (an "&" count), that eighth note is immediately preceded or followed by another bell that does fall on a beat. The ringer now has an "anchor" around which to ring the eighth notes. This is wise planning, especially when making assignments for beginners. *Plan for success!*

As admitted earlier, we do mark our music for the ringers. We even color-code the music for our ringers, but this has absolutely nothing to do with the way we assign bells or the way we think through the assigning process. However, the fact that the music is marked in color does make it much easier to see the assignment possibilities. It also necessitates buying a copy of music for each ringer, but other directors have developed ways of marking so that two ringers can share one copy of music. For those who may be interested, in chapter 8 I will describe our color-coding method.

In assigning music for four or five octaves of bells, I would recommend distributing the low bells first because their size and weight can make them more difficult to assign than the high bells. As a matter of convenience, at the top of each page of music we write the names of the bells assigned to that position in that piece of music. Because we color-code our music, we do this in color also.

A Word of Caution: For some ringers, especially beginning ringers, executing two different techniques at the same time is very difficult. Try not to make an assignment that requires ringers to ring one bell while shaking another.

A Word to the Wise: If more than two bells are assigned to a ringing position, clearly indicate which two bells are used first. This will save many false starts!

Sharing Bells

If two (or more) ringers are to share bells, indicate this at the top of the first page of music for each ringer involved. Some directors do this by enclosing the names of the shared bells in either brackets or parentheses. For example, if ringer #1 and ringer #2 are to share D#4, the music would be marked this way:

♪ Ringer #1 (D#4): Indicates that D#4 begins at this ringing position.

♪ Ringer #2 [D#4]: Indicates that D#4 begins at another position and will come to this ringing position.

Rather than use brackets and parentheses, we write specific information about sharing bells. For example, if ringer #1 began with D#4 and then passed that bell to ringer #2, at the top of ringer #1's music we would write: "D#4 starts here, goes to ringer #2." On ringer #2's music we would write: "(D#4 coming from ringer #1)."

After all the bells have been assigned, on the first page of each piece of music we draw a "game plan" or "table plan" for that ringing position. This chart tells the ringer what to expect initially in the way of bell changes. It cannot show every bell change that will need to be made, but it will help him arrange his bells in the most convenient and logical way. Here is a sample game plan or table plan:

GAME PLAN or TABLE PLAN

C4	D4
C#4	D#4
G3	D7

As you look at this chart, the names of the bells listed to the left of the vertical line are to be rung with the left hand; the bells to the right of the line are to be rung with the right hand. For each hand, the bells are listed from top to bottom in order of their use and in the order the first changes occur. If a bell is rung first with the left hand and then with the right hand, an arrow indicates the hand-swap and the chart would look like this:

GAME PLAN or TABLE PLAN

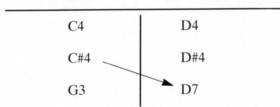

C4	D4
C#4	D#4
G3	D7

On the music, at the places where bell changes are to occur, we write instructions for these changes, telling the ringer which bells to put down and which ones to pick up. We also tell the ringers when and with whom they are to share bells. The instructions written on the music would look like this:

♪ C down/C# up (this could be abbreviated C/C# if such a system were established)

♪ D7 coming from #1 (after the bell was used, "Return D7 to #1")

♪ Give D7 to #2 (after the bell was used, "D7 returned from #2")

(See chapter 8 for an example.)

*Whatever system you use to indicate bell changes and bell shar-
ing, be sure your ringers understand it!*

Placing Information on the Director's Score

Once all the bells are assigned, somewhere on the director's
score, I provide the following types of information that will be
valuable when assigning ringers to the ringing positions and when
rehearsing the piece of music:

♪ On the handbells used chart, indicate the bell
  distribution/assignments.

♪ Indicate which ringing positions will be difficult and challenging.

♪ Indicate which ringing positions are the easiest.

♪ Indicate places in the music where special techniques may
  cause difficulties.

♪ Indicate where the fifth-octave bass bells must be rung with
  one hand. This lets the director know to place at those positions ringers capable of ringing the heavy bass bells.

♪ If the ringers do not always remain at the same positions,
  give any information that would be helpful in placing specific
  ringers at specific ringing positions.

Bell Passing Slips

To help us move floater bells and prepare for another piece of
music, we use bell passing slips, or what the ringers call "cheat
sheets." These slips are placed in the ringers' notebooks *before*
the piece of music they effect and they show where the floater
bells will be placed in the upcoming piece. These slips are not
full-page size, but are just large enough to accommodate all the
necessary information. By writing crosswise on a piece of paper,
three or four of these information slips can be put on one page
and the entire page duplicated. Then holes for the notebook are
punched in each bell-passing slip. All bell-passing slips are kept
on file and reused every time that piece of music is rung in worship or concert. Besides allowing the ringers to move quickly

from piece to piece, by using these slips *before* each piece of music, the order in which the pieces of music are rung can be varied at any time and the system will still work. The following is an example of a bell passing slip:

"SELECTION #2"	
Floater Bells	**Ringer**
LOW BELLS	
C3	#1
F3	#3
G3	#3
A3	#4
B♭3	#5
HIGH BELLS	
D7	#4
E♭7	#6
E7	#11
G7	#12
C8	#1

Here is how the bell passing slips work:
  ♪ The slip shows where the floater bells will be rung in "Selection #2" (the music immediately following the bell passing slip).
  ♪ After ringing "Selection #1" the ringer turns to this bell passing slip for "Selection #2."
  ♪ The ringer looks at the slip to see if any of the floater bells she has just finished using for "Selection #1" will be used in "Selection #2."
  ♪ If any are to be used, she *takes* the bells to the positions where they will be needed for "Selection #2."
  ♪ If any of the bells are not needed for "Selection #2," she returns those bells to the cases or table where the floater bells are kept when not in use.
  ♪ If a ringer needs a bell for "Selection #2" and it is not immediately brought to her, she knows that it wasn't used in the previous piece, "Selection #1," and she gets it from the case or table where the floater bells are kept.

When working with children's bell choirs, the music will not be as complex, there will not be many floater bells, and the information will not be lengthy, so on these bell passing slips I also list the ringing positions and the name of the ringer assigned to each position. Since these are ringer-specific, they are not kept on file or reused.

File Cards of Bell Assignments

As a matter of convenience for myself, I also keep a card file of the bell assignments for all the music in our handbell library. This makes it possible to find information about the bell assignments for any piece of music without having to take the director's score from the music library or from his or her music notebook. It is also a "back-up" in case music is misfiled or lost. The following is a sample card:

TITLE _____

COMPOSER_____OCTAVES____

#0 - #1 - #2 - #3 - #4 - #5 - #6 - #7 - #8 - #9 - #10 - #11 - #12 -

The information on these cards can be very helpful if a ringer is absent from rehearsal and he or she took the music home to study or memorize. Because we color-code our music, the information on our cards is recorded in the same colors. Bell assignment information can also be stored in a computer, but we are still at the paper-and-colored-pen stage!

Chapter Six
Concepts of Good Bell Assignments

I once heard a handbell director tell a concert audience to watch the ringer on the far right. "She doesn't have anything to do but ring on the last chord!" he said. At the other extreme, I have often been distracted by the ringer (usually in the bass bells!) who looks like an octopus because he has far too much to do and cannot ring all the bells assigned to him. In both of these examples, the director has violated what I consider to be the cardinal rule of handbell assignments:

Good bell assignments should not draw attention to any ringer!

Assigning for Success

FALL 199

As stated in chapter 4:
- ♪ Good bell assignments facilitate accurate ringing and damping.
- ♪ Good bell assignments should be possible, practical, and logical.
- ♪ Good bell assignments will solve problems before ringers experience them.
- ♪ Good bell assignments will allow the ringer to ring every note for every bell assigned to the position.
- ♪ Once the music is learned, ringers should be able to ring their parts correctly 99 percent of the time.
- ♪ Ringers should be physically capable of ringing the assignments.
- ♪ Consider the size and weight of the low bells.
- ♪ Allow ample time for the ringer to make the required changes.

♪ Assign all bells before introducing the music to the bell choir. Do not waste valuable rehearsal time asking, "Who can ring G7?"

♪ Remove difficult-to-ring bells before the ringers "lay claim" to them.

♪ Negates the concept: "These are my bells!"

♪ Negates the concept: "I can ring them all!"

♪ Teaches that the Christian way is to share.

Admittedly, sometimes an assignment works better on paper than it does on the bells, so when ringers make improvements in their assignments, they should share this information with the director. The director should be flexible and open to these changes, making note of them so that they can be shared with ringers who will be ringing the assignments in the future.

As you plan your bell assignments, consider these factors:

♪ Age of the ringers

♪ Ability level of the ringers, individually and as a group

♪ Level of understanding

♪ Level of coordination

♪ Size and physical strength of ringers

♪ Visual and physical problems (especially of older ringers)

Deciding Where to Assign Floater Bells

Assigning bells is much like working a jigsaw puzzle. When the work is done, all the pieces fit together to form a complete picture, there are no missing pieces, and there are no pieces left over. Some people work puzzles in a haphazard way, hoping for the right outcome. Others are very organized in the way they separate shapes and colors. When assigning bells, I want to be organized, to plan ahead, and to be certain that, when I am finished, I do not have one bell that no one can ring. Determining the best places to assign floater bells takes thought and planning, but it also takes practice.

FALL 199

As you plan the placement of floater bells, keep these ideas in mind:

Availability: Sometimes *only one ringer* can handle the floater bell. Assign it to him. Sometimes a ringer could musically handle *only one floater bell.* Give her priority.

Keep ringers busy: Sometimes a ringer needs more to do to keep her busy.

Rhythmic problems: Sometimes a bell needs to be assigned to a specific ringer to help handle special or difficult rhythmic problems.

Last chord: It is always nice to ring on the last chord. Often there will be a floater bell that could be assigned to a ringer so that he can ring on the last chord. This keeps him attentive and involved until the end of the piece. It also helps keep him out of trouble!

Sharing bells: We pass and share bells when it is necessary. However, we try to place all bells where they can be handled by the same ringer throughout the entire piece of music. If this is not possible, we try to make the bell-sharing consistent, simple, and logical.

Who can do the best job? All things considered, assign all bells to those who can ring them accurately and in the most musical way.

Have a plan: Look for problems. Find solutions. Do what works best for you and your ringers.

Techniques and Aspects of Ringing that Can Cause Assignment Problems

Rules for Ringing "Right"

♪ One hand should not ring two different bells on two consecutive beats.

♪ Consider the size and weight of the bells when asking for quick bell changes.

Watch for These Techniques

The following techniques, which can cause assignment difficulties, are defined and further explained in chapter 9.

Staccato Passages: In handbell music, staccato passages are normally played using one of the techniques listed below. The technique used depends on the size of the bell and/or the indication given by the composer. There is a slightly different sound produced by each of these ways of executing a staccato note, so ringers should try to follow the composer's indications. However, working for a uniform sound in the staccato line sometimes necessitates substituting one method of playing a staccato note for another on some of the bells.

♪ **Thumb Damp:** Used on the smaller bells. It's difficult for ringers to change quickly from ringing to thumb damping.

♪ **Pluck:** Most often used on medium-to-large bells. Ringers must be taught not to try to pluck every bell with the same hand. Ringers have two hands and we must presume that they both work! Teach ringers to use both hands alternately to pluck a succession of bells.

♪ **Hand Damp:** Used on medium-to-large bells when the thumb and one or two fingers are not sufficient to create a staccato effect. Ringers need one hand to hold and ring the bell. The other hand must be free to be placed on the bell casting as the bell is rung.

♪ **Mallets:** A mallet of the proper weight and size may be used on any bell. (When used to strike a bell on the outside of the casting near the lip of the bell, at approximately the same place the clapper strikes the inside of the bell, a mallet should produce approximately the same sound as the clapper, on the soft setting, when it strikes the inside of the bell. See chapter 2.) Sometimes the composer offers the option of plucking the bells or placing them on the table and striking the bell casting with a mallet. Using a mallet on the bells rather than plucking them enables a ringer to perform a staccato passage quickly, cleanly, and accurately.

Quick Changes from One Technique to Another: Any change in ringing techniques has the potential for causing assignment problems. Make assignments that will allow the ringers time to change from one technique to another.

Chromatic Passages: These passages have a great potential for causing assignment problems. First identify the bells that are causing the problem. Of those bells, try to select the bell that is least used in the piece of music and reassign that bell to another ringer.

Enharmonics: If enharmonics are to be shared by ringers, be certain that each ringer can handle every note he or she should ring. (We don't assume that ringers will always be able to share bells and cover all enharmonic changes. We indicate on the music when and where to share bells with neighbor ringers.) Watch key changes and chords with accidentals. Sometimes just one chord can cause havoc with bell assignments!

LV (Let Vibrate) Passages: Assignment problems caused by these passages are easy to overlook. In an LV section, a bell must be allowed to sound longer than its written note value. This means that the ringer must keep the bell in-hand, sometimes preventing him from making a bell change within his normal assignment. A ringer will often have two bells involved in the LV passage, further complicating normal bell changes. Watch all LV sections for potential assignment problems.

Mallets on Suspended Bells: A ringer must hold a bell in one hand and have the other hand free to hold and use the mallet. Sometimes it is necessary to hold two or more bells in one hand so each bell may be struck with the mallet and then allowed to continue to sound. Getting bells and mallet into position requires time. Bells struck in this way usually are not damped.

Tricky Rhythmic Passages: Always put tricky rhythmic passages into the hands of the fewest ringers possible. This may necessitate sharing bells, but it will help the ringers perform the passages smoothly. Ringers must be able to count passages correctly before they can ring them correctly. Have ringers verbalize rhythms:

♪ Eighth notes = apple
♪ Triplets = peppermint, chocolate, butterfly, one-lol-ly, two-lol-ly, and so on
♪ Sixteenth notes = huckleberry
♪ Grace notes = dee DUM
♪ Quarter/dotted eighth and sixteenth/quarter = Here/comes the/bride

Passing the Assignment Test

Ringers should not have to invent "techniques" to solve ringing problems that directors have created with poor bell assignments!

You have passed the assignment test if:
♪ All bells are assigned.
♪ All assignments are workable/feasible.
♪ The entire bell choir rings accurately.
♪ The entire bell choir damps accurately. (Damping is just as important as ringing and should be just as accurate as ringing.)
♪ The ringers can produce a musical performance using the assignments you have given them.

Chapter Seven
The First Rehearsal

A t this point in your career as a handbell director, you are probably working with a group of "wannabees". Your job is to transform this group of want-to-be-ringers into a handbell choir. Sometimes this takes a lot of prayer, patience, and a few near miracles! The following suggestions for the first rehearsal will help you get started on the "right foot" (or in this case, on the right hand!).

Let the Ringers Know What Is Expected of Them

The first rehearsal is the time and place to lay the ground rules, regardless of the age of the ringers. Formulate your policies and share with your ringers what you expect of them regarding:
- ♪ Attendance/on-time policies
- ♪ Care of bells
- ♪ Gloves (to wear or not to wear)
- ♪ Respect for bells, equipment, director, fellow ringers, church/school
- ♪ Discipline/self-discipline

Some directors create an application/information form for the ringers to complete. In addition to names, parents' names (they are often different), spouses' names, addresses, and phone numbers, you can also ask if the ringers play a musical instrument, where they go to school/work, if they are involved in sports, scouting, or other extracurricular activities, what special interests they have, and so on.

For our children's bell choirs, we have a commitment letter that must be signed by the ringer and at least one parent. We keep the signed letters on file in case we need to remind the ringer or parent of the commitment that was made. It is not too early to teach the children (and hopefully not too late to teach the parents) the importance of honoring commitments and being true to your word. Our letter details what is expected of the ringers who accept the responsibility of being a part of the handbell choir for the current school year. We put in writing all the expectations that were discussed at the first rehearsal. We list some of the "excuses" a ringer might have for missing rehearsal, plainly stating that birthday parties, ball games, or staying home to blow dry your parakeet, are not acceptable reasons for missing bell choir! The only acceptable reasons are sickness or death. All of us know that there are other acceptable reasons, but we would prefer to deal with those reasons on an individual basis as they occur. If ringers or their families have regular activities that would cause the ringers to miss bell choir, we suggest that they not participate in the bell choir that year. We have found that it is far better to begin with strict rules and relax or bend them as necessary than it is to try to "get tough" when the situation gets out of control. Make sure that the rules you make for your ringers are fair, consistent, consistently enforced, and that everyone understands them and the consequences of breaking them.

Everyone responds to praise.
- ♪ Find something to praise!
- ♪ Expect good work. Expect the ringer's best.
- ♪ Be realistic in your expectations. (Sometimes you have to be thankful for the right notes!)
- ♪ Encourage your ringers.
- ♪ Understand your ringers and their capabilities whatever their age or skill level.

Now that you have learned the philosophies, the theories, and the how-to's, you are ready to see how they can be put into practice with "live" ringers and bells!

Teaching the Basics of Ringing

Today, many directors who work with American-made handbells prefer to have the clappers adjusted so that there is uneven tension on the restraining springs. This means that the clapper will more easily strike the bell on one side of the casting than on the other, usually on the side that is opposite the manufacturer's logo. (The logo is found on only one side of the handle, just below the handguard.) If the clapper springs are adjusted with uneven tension, this logo should be up when the bell is on the table and toward the ringer when the bell is in-hand. Some directors prefer to have equal tension on the restraining springs. This means that the bell will ring with equal ease on either side. (This is our preference.) Consult the manufacturer's instructions to learn how to adjust the restraining springs to suit your preferences and needs. With this information ready to share with the ringers, you are now ready to begin teaching them to ring.

It is far more difficult to tell someone how to hold and ring a bell correctly than it is to show how it should be done.
Try to visualize this:

♪ Hold the bell as you would an ice cream cone or a tennis racquet.

♪ Firmly grasp the handle beneath the circular handguard.

♪ The bell clapper should move perpendicular to your body.

♪ If the clapper springs are adjusted with uneven tension, lift the bell so that the side of the handle with the bell emblem or logo is toward your body.

♪ Lift the bell to an upright position and tilt it back slightly so the clapper rests toward the side of the bell nearest your shoulder. This is called the ready-to-ring position.

♪ Normally you should ring the bell above your waist and below your shoulder.

♪ The correct ringing motion is oval or football-shaped.

♪ From the ready-to-ring position at your shoulder, move the bell slightly downward and outward.

♪ At the outermost point of the football-shaped motion, snap or flick your wrist to make the bell ring.

♪ Continue the motion, bringing the bell slightly upward and back to your shoulder.

♪ The bell may then be damped (silenced) against your shoulder.

♪ After damping the bell, move it slightly away from your shoulder and into the ready-to-ring position.

♪ The quicker the notes to be rung, the smaller the football-shaped motion must be.

♪ Very fast passages may be rung by little more than a snap of the wrist at shoulder level. The bell can then be damped quickly if necessary.

No matter how well you think you have explained the correct ringing motion, there will always be someone who "just doesn't get it!" The concept of moving the bell downward, outward, upward, and backward in a football-shaped motion seems very descriptive to me, especially when the verbal explanation is accompanied by a demonstration of the correct motion. In one seminar I led, I thought I had done a very good job explaining and demonstrating this motion. When I finished and asked if there were any questions, one woman raised her hand and asked, "At which point of the *basketball* did you say to snap your wrist?"

Practicing the Correct Ringing Motion

Practicing without bells: Have your ringers practice the correct motion without having bells in their hands. Ringers can get the feel of the correct motion, the director can check each ringer's motion, and the sound of bells ringing is not interfering with the director's instructions.

Practicing with "silent bells": Today's ringers would call them "air bells"! Let the ringers have bells in hand, but tell them not to make the bells sound. Practice the ringing motion, but do not snap the wrists, and do not make the bells sound.

Random ringing: Now allow the ringers to make their bells ring. Let them work independently, getting the feel of the bell and the correct motion, but make no attempt to get them to ring together. When ringers have difficulty, stand behind them, letting them hold the bell, grasp their hand in yours and make the correct motion with them. Children will naturally tend to do things the easy way. Adults will try to make it difficult! Be patient with them regardless of their age.

Ringing together: Ringers must follow instructions and they must follow the director. At your direction, ask them to ring whatever bell they have in their right hand five times. (The rhythmic pattern you should direct is four quarter notes followed by one whole note.) Warn them that what they hear will sound discordant, not like music, and ask them to try to make all of the bells ring at exactly the same time. Repeat this process using the bells in their left hand. After doing each of these exercises several times, ask them to alternate hands. Start the pattern first with the right hand; then start the pattern with the left hand.

Ringing chords: A simple way to do this verbally is to call out the letter names of the bells to be rung.

Say: C E G / Ring D F A / Ring E G B /Ring F A C /Ring
Conduct: 1   2 3 4   1   2 3 4   1   2 3 4   1

Perhaps a better way is to use cards with one chord (triad) written on each card. The cards must be large enough and the markings bold enough to be seen across the rehearsal room.

G	A	B	C	D
E	F	G	A	B
C	D	E	F	G

1 2 3 4 / 1 2 3 4 / 1 2 3 4 / 1 2 3 4 / 1 2 3 4

Continue this process until you cover the entire octave. You would also need cards for these chords: A, C, E; B, D, F; and a second C, E, G card to complete the octave. As soon as the ringers have rung the chord, while you continue to count aloud, take away the card they have just rung and show them the next card. You should give them as much time as possible to prepare to ring the next chord.

Repeated chords: Now show the ringers one of the cards and ask them to ring that chord five times. You can vary the number of

times the chord is to be rung, and you can vary the dynamic
levels you ask them to ring. Try this:

♪ Have them ring five chords, gradually getting louder. (Hold
the last chord.)

♪ Have them ring five chords, gradually getting softer. (Hold
the last chord.)

♪ Have them ring four chords that gradually get louder and five
chords that gradually get softer. (Hold the last chord.)

Damping: Up until now, as we have practiced these exercises with
the ringers, we have not even mentioned damping. We have
only stopped the sound of the last chord of an exercise. Show
the ringers how to touch the lip of the bell to their shoulder to
damp or stop its sound. (Explain to children that the word you
are using has a "p" at the end of it! You are not saying a bad
word!) Notice that the correct word is *damp,* not *dampen.*
Dampen means "to wet." Damp means "to stop the sound."
Show the ringers what happens when bells are damped correctly.

♪ The bell that is sounding is damped just as the next bell is
rung—not too early and not too late.

Also show the ringers what happens when bells are incorrectly
damped.

♪ Damping too late makes the sounds run together and sound
messy.

♪ Damping too soon leaves a "hole" in the sound. The notes
aren't connected.

*Do not make a big issue of damping at this time. Correct damp-
ing will come with time and practice.*

Exercises Using R's and L's

Although the following exercises could be written on a marker
board, it is nice to put them on reusable charts. Have the ringers
use whatever bells are in front of them on the tables.

In each of the exercises you will find:

♪ R = red = right hand

♪ L = blue = left hand

♪ Numbers represent counts on which bells are to be rung. In the first example, the ringers ring only on the first count of each measure. Then they have three counts to think about what to do next! Ask them to begin trying to damp each bell at exactly the same time they ring the next bell.

Example 1

```
4  R          / L          / R          / L          /
4  1  2  3  4 / 1  2  3  4 / 1  2  3  4 / 1  2  3  4 /

   R          / R          / L          / L          /
   1  2  3  4 / 1  2  3  4 / 1  2  3  4 / 1  2  3  4 /
```

In Example 2, ringers now have to make quicker responses, ringing on the first and third counts of each measure. In this example, the dashes mean to let the bell continue to sound. Continue to work on damping.

Example 2

```
4 R __ R __ / L __ L __ / R __ L __ / L __ R __ /
4 1  2  3  4/ 1  2 3 4 / 1  2  3  4/ 1 2  3  4 /
```

The L's and R's in the next exercise indicate that ringers are to ring on every count of each measure. Ask them to damp their left-hand bell at exactly the same time they ring their right-hand bell and vice versa.

Example 3

```
4  R  R  R  R / L  L  L  L / R  R  R  R / R  L  R  L /
4  1  2  3  4 / 1  2  3  4 / 1  2  3  4 / 1  2  3  4 /

   R  L  R  L / R  R  L  R / L  L  R  L / R  R  R  L /
   1  2  3  4 / 1  2  3  4 / 1  2  3  4 / 1  2  3  4 /

   L  R  R  L / L  L  L  R / L  L  L  L / R  R  R  R /
   1  2  3  4 / 1  2  3  4 / 1  2  3  4 / 1  2  3  4 /
```

In the last example in this section, an "x" represents a count on which nothing is rung. In the middle of the exercise it also indicates damping.

Example 4

```
4  x  x  R  x  /  x  R  x  R  /  x  L  x  L  /  L  x  x  R  /
4  1  2  3  4  /  1  2  3  4  /  1  2  3  4  /  1  2  3  4  /
```

If you choose to color-code the music using our system detailed in chapter 8, and if you use the standard distribution of two diatonic notes per ringer, when you mark the ringers' music, the space notes will be circled in blue and the line notes will be circled in red. Even if you do not use the standard distribution, the bells/notes rung with the left hand can be marked in blue and the bells/notes rung with the right hand can be marked in red.

Creating Exercises from the Printed Music

After using the above exercises as an introduction to ringing, you can create your own exercises from the music being learned. Isolate a passage that may be a problem for only one ringer and from it create an exercise for all the ringers to practice. In so doing, you may prevent the problem and you will certainly prevent calling attention to any one ringer's problems. Try this:

Clapping Rhythms   *FALL '99*

♪ Introduce new rhythmic patterns by having all ringers clap the patterns before trying to ring them. ·
♪ Have all ringers clap rhythmic patterns that may cause problems for one particular ringer.

Speaking Rhythms

♪ Have all ringers speak (or count aloud) the new rhythmic pattern.

♪ If desired, replace the counting with appropriate word phrases that will help the ringers to verbalize the rhythms. (See information on tricky rhythmic patterns in chapter 6.)

First Use of Printed Music

Each director will have to decide when to use printed music with the ringers. We like to do this near the end of the first rehearsal, and we select music that the ringers will recognize. Our goal is to have them go home having rung a real piece of music at the very first rehearsal!

When you put the first piece of music before the ringers, you need to explain to them what they will see. They need to know something about these elements of music:

♪ Lines and spaces
♪ Treble and bass clefs
♪ The grand staff
♪ Note values
  ♪ Whole notes
  ♪ Half notes
  ♪ Quarter notes

Also explain to the ringers these important nonmusical elements:

♪ Any markings you may have placed on the music
♪ Your method of indicating which bells to pick up first

Working with Beginners of All Ages

There is a tendency to think that beginners means children, but this is not necessarily true. Beginners may be children, youth, or adults. However, when working with children, you might want to have parents attend the first rehearsal. You then have the opportunity to:

♪ Meet the children's parents (if you do not already know them).
♪ Open a line of communication with parents and their children.

♪ Show them how vital it is for you and the handbell program to have their support.

♪ Include them in the information and instructions you give the ringers.

♪ Involve parents in some of the early activities you introduce to the ringers.

Much of the success in working with children depends on the support you receive from their parents. Children are dependent on their parents to bring them to rehearsals and performances. In today's society, children whose families are affected by divorce or parental separation often spend the weekdays with one parent and the weekends with another. In these situations, it is vitally important that both parents/families realize the importance of the child's attendance at bell choir rehearsals and activities.

Regardless of the age of the bell choir, I would begin in the same way. I would alter the language used so it would be appropriate for the age group, and I would expect faster progress from beginning youth ringers than I would from either beginning children or adult ringers. Sometimes children do not have the motor skills to do what they mentally understand. Youth usually have the mental ability and the motor skills to both understand the concepts and execute the motions. Adults also have these intellectual and motor skills, but as they get older, they may lose some of their physical strength, coordination, and endurance. Also, they do not react as quickly as they did in their younger years. Children and youth are anxious to try new things. Adults are more cautious, sometimes fearful of embarrassing themselves.

No matter what the age of the ringers, the director must put them at ease. Let them know that it is normal to make mistakes, but that they should learn from their mistakes. Let them know that you do not expect perfection, but you do expect their very best, whatever that may be.

Chapter Eight
Red/Right—Blue/Left
(Color-Coding Music)

Those who have rung in our bell choirs know that in our color-coding system, *red* indicates the *right hand, blue* indicates the *left hand.* Recently I was the organist for the wedding of one of our former ringers. When the time came for the exchange of rings, from my vantage point I could see that the groom let the bride try to put the ring on his *right hand.* At the reception I kidded him about it and he said, "If the minister had said to put the ring on my *blue hand* I would have known which hand he meant!"

As musicians, it is difficult to put ourselves in the place of one who cannot read music. It is hard for most of us to remember not being able to read, and many of us have trouble remembering not being able to read music because we have known how for such a long time. Learning to read music compares to learning a foreign language. Another analogy I can make is trying to become "computer literate" after the age of fifty! I can read the manual, I know the words, but since I do not understand the context I really cannot understand the manual. This is very annoying when I want to use the computer now and see results immediately! It is very humbling! Ringers who look at music but cannot read it must feel the same way. In learning new languages and new skills, all of us must gradually learn the basics. One reason for color-coding handbell music is to allow the ringers to see immediate results and experience some degree of success while gradually learning the basics of music reading.

Since we are musicians we should easily be able to read the following piece of music from an Arabic hymnal. We should be able to sing it, play it on the piano, and/or ring it with a bell choir. We can read music and we can read words, so we should not have any problems! All we have to do is read from right to left (this is not a mirror image). If we lose our place in the music, we can always follow the words. Try it!

	١
والكَـــرى ســـائِـدان"	في الدُجَى والسُّكــون"
ساجِــدان يَـهـران"	يوسفُ ومَـــريـــمُ
نَـــامَ بِـأمَــان"	ويسُـــوعُ الطِفَـــلُ

	٢
في الدُجى والسُّكون"	في السَّمَــا للرِعَـاة
بجُـــور يُنْشِـدون"	جيشُ جنـدٍ ظهَـروا
ربُّنَــا الحَنـــون"	وُلِــدَ المسِــحُ

	٣
خالِــدةٌ وعظيــمٌ	ليلــةٌ ذِكـرُهَـا
نِعمَــةُ الربِّ الكريم"	إذْ تَجَلَّتْ للـــورى
مُفتَــدي الاثيـــمُ	في وجْهِ المسِـح

How did you do? It is not as easy as you thought, is it? Did you recognize the music as "Silent Night"? You will need a group of ringers or parents to help you with the next one. In the following example you will find the text to Psalm 135 and you will find a vocabulary list (comparable to a handbells used chart). Everyone in the group must have a copy of the example. Before going any further, explain to them these rules:

♪ **No one is to write anything.**

♪ Read only your assigned word(s). (You have to remember your words.)

♪ Read aloud at a good pace.
♪ **No one is to write anything.**

Reading *down* each column of vocabulary words, go around the group, assigning each person one word. When everyone has one word, go around again and assign each person another word. Continue this process until all the vocabulary words are assigned. If the group is small, the participants will have several words to remember and the exercise can be difficult. Once again remind the group of the rules, then ask them to read the psalm.

VOCABULARY LIST

Praise	ye	the
Lord	name	of
Him	O	servants
that	stand	in
house	courts	our
God	for	is
good	sing	unto
his	it	pleasant

PSALM 135:1-3

Praise ye the Lord. Praise ye the name of the Lord;
praise him, O ye servants of the Lord.
Ye that stand in the house of the Lord,
in the courts of the house of our God,
Praise the Lord; for the Lord is good:
sing praises unto his name;
for it is pleasant. (KJV)

Groups rarely complete the first line without falling apart! They cannot remember their word(s), someone forgets to read, the reading is uneven and disjointed, and there is always one who did not understand the instructions! Sounds just like a bell choir! Now try the same exercise again, allowing ringers to mark their vocabulary words and circle those words every time they appear in the psalm. You will be amazed at how much the reading improves. Sounds just like a bell choir reading marked music!

Reasons for Color-Coding

The following are our primary reasons for color-coding music for our bell choirs:

♪ More people can participate in the handbell program.

♪ The music is uniformly marked for all ringers and all choirs.

♪ Marking helps the ringer isolate the assigned notes.

We do teach the basics of music notation and music reading, but we do not require this knowledge for a person to be allowed to participate in a bell choir. If we are honest with ourselves, learning to read music is not the real reason ringers come to bell choir. They come because of the camaraderie, the fellowship, the mutual support, the physical exercise, and for the fun and enjoyment of it all. Some ring bass bells for a workout in lieu of going to the gym! Some of the adults say bell choir is their weekly therapy!

Directors who require ringers to read music often have permanent ringing positions for their ringers, that is, a ringer is assigned the same position for the entire year. If the director assigns bells using the standard distribution of two diatonic notes per ringer, a ringer quickly learns to ring the space notes with her left hand and the line notes with her right hand. Ringers are learning to read "their" notes, but they are not necessarily learning to read the full score.

By their very nature, ringing assignments are fragmented. Many of us can read the entire score easier than we can isolate our assigned notes. What other instrument is expected to extract its individual part from the full score? Marking music, in whatever way chosen, helps ringers isolate their notes.

There are also reasons for not using our system of color-coding music:

♪ Marking requires time on the part of the director.

♪ The system is based on a set number of ringers per choir.

♪ Marking requires purchasing a copy of music for each ringer.

We make no apologies for our system of marking because it works for us! However, we respect others' decisions not to mark or color-code their music. Make your own decision. If you decide to color-code your ringers' music, do it without guilt. Do what works for you and your choir!

Looking at Color-Coded Music

Please refer to the musical example on page 72, "Jesus' Hands Were Kind Hands," as you read the following explanation of color-coding.

If you were to look at a piece of bell music that had been color-coded for one of our ringing positions, here is what you would see.

♪ The names of the bells assigned to that part are written in color at the top of each page of music.

♪ Each bell is identified (and its notes marked in the score) by a different color.

   ♪ The colors identify specific bells in a given piece.

   ♪ The colors may change from piece to piece.

♪ Each ringer has one bell (pitch) marked in blue, one marked in red, and perhaps others marked in green, pink, or another color.

♪ Of the position's regularly assigned bells, the one to be rung with the left hand is marked in blue; the one to be rung with the right hand is marked in red.

♪ On the staff, the notes are circled in the appropriate colors.

♪ The counts on which the note is to be rung are written in the same color. (The rest of the counting is written in pencil or pen.)

♪ A colored line is drawn after the note (in the staff) to indicate how long the bell (note) is to sound.

   ♪ Sometimes the line is an indication of the note's value.

   ♪ Sometimes the line identifies an LV passage.

   ♪ The line helps prevent premature damping (especially for beginning ringers).

♪ Two bells that are to be rung simultaneously have these markings:

   ♪ Each note is circled in the appropriate color.

   ♪ The count on which the bells are to be rung is written in one of the colors.

   ♪ There is a circle around the colored count and the circle is the color of the second bell to be rung on that count.

Example of Marked Music

Jesus' Hands Were Kind Hands

TRADITIONAL FRENCH
Arranged by Martha Lynn Thompson

Color Coordination

Not only is our music color-coded, it is color coordinated!
♪ Left hand = blue/green/purple
♪ Right hand = red/pink/orange
♪ Bells that change hands = yellow

The primary bell rung with the left hand is marked in blue. When that bell is exchanged for another bell, the second bell would be marked in green, the next in purple, and so on, always using colors in the same color family.

The primary bell rung with the right hand is marked in red. If that bell is exchanged for another bell, the second bell would be marked in pink, the next in orange, and so on, always using colors in this color family.

Bells that move from one hand to another are marked in yellow because it does not look like either of the other two color families. Sometimes yellow can be difficult to see, but it is a color that can be seen by color-blind people. We have had color-blind ringers and they have all used our color-coding system quite successfully.

When bell changes are necessary, the changes are written *beneath* the system of music. The changes are *written in the colors* of the bells involved. We write "C down/C# up," but this could be abbreviated as C/C# or in a variety of other effective ways. These instructions would appear immediately after C had been rung for the last time, no matter how long it would be before the C# is used.

Critics of this system have said that we do not need music, we just need colored counts! That could be true, but it would be impractical and we would not recommend it. We make a game of finding unmarked notes. We tell the ringers that they will get $1,000,000 if they find an unmarked note! Some even try to collect half that if they find the note marked but the count not marked! It is surprising how many unmarked notes these non-music-reading ringers find, but it is even more amazing how many trained musicians do not find or ring any unmarked notes!

Even if our ringers are reading color-coded music, they are learning a lot about music. They are also learning valuable lessons that have absolutely nothing to do with music. There will be more about that important aspect of ringing in later chapters.

Chapter Nine
Notational Devices for
Handbell Techniques

Music selected for the beginning bell choir should use the basic straight-ringing technique most of the time, but as the ringers progress, they will want to learn other ringing techniques. They will encounter symbols and notational devices that they will need to know how to interpret in handbell music. Some of these symbols are commonly used in music notation, but they have special and specific meaning in handbell literature. Once the ringers master the basic stroke, gradually introduce the following symbols, teach the meaning of each symbol, and show the ringers how to perform the technique represented by each symbol.

Ring or R: Either symbol indicates ringing the bell in the normal way. **R** is often used to indicate a return to normal ringing after another technique has been used. At the beginning of a piece of music, even without "Ring" or "R," all bells are to be rung unless otherwise indicated.

Damp: Stop the sound of the bell by touching it to the shoulder, to a padded table, or with a gloved hand. The damp sign ⊕ indicates the damping of all bells sounding.

LV (Let Vibrate or *Laissez Vibrer*): Let bells continue to sound, disregarding note values and rests. An LV section may be ended by a damp sign, by the indication of a new LV, by the use of another technique, or by "Ring" or "R."

Shake, SK or 〰〰〰 : The bell is shaken rapidly, making the clapper strike both sides of the bell. Shakes may be indicated by either or both symbols. Common ways of indicating shakes and their interpretations are as follows:

   1. **SK** 〰 Normal unbroken shake.
   2. **o** 〰〰〰 **o** 〰〰〰 or **o** 〰〰〰'**o** 〰〰〰

Stop the shake just short of the value of the first note, restrike the note and continue the shake for the value of the second note.

3. **o ⌢⌢⌢ o ⌢⌢⌢** A continuous shake for the value of both notes.

Swing or SW or ↓ ↑: After ringing the bell in the normal way, it is swung to the side of the body, first downward then upward. Arrows may be used to indicate the direction of the swing and the counts on which it occurs. Remember to ring the bell before swinging it!

Thumb Damp or TD: With the thumb or thumb and forefinger on the bell casting, ring the bell in the normal way. This produces a staccato sound. This technique is used on smaller bells when a pluck is not possible or practical.

Pluck or PL: With the bell on a padded table, manually "flip" the clapper to strike the bell casting. This makes a short, staccato sound. When used on medium to large bells, the clapper is flipped downward. When a ringer lifts the clapper in preparation for a pluck on these larger bells, his thumb must be positioned on top of the clapper (at twelve o'clock), and his second and third fingers positioned at the bottom of the clapper (at about six o'clock). When this is done, the left wrist will be at about ten o'clock and the right wrist at about two o'clock. The clapper is then flipped straight downward (toward six o'clock) and released. Steadying the bell is unnecessary because the downward thrust of the clapper prevents the bell from rolling sideways. When smaller bells are plucked, the ringer should place one or two fingers on the end of the clapper or beneath the clapper and flip it upward. Bells plucked in this manner need to be steadied.

Martellato or ▼: The bell is sounded by holding it by the handle and *gently* striking the *full body of the casting* horizontally into a properly padded table. This produces a forceful and dramatic sound.

Martellato Lift or ▼↑ : After sounding the bell using the martellato technique described above, the bell is immediately lifted to allow it to continue to sound.

WARNING: Improper use of these martellato techniques may

cause damage to the handbell casting. On bells G3 and below, use another technique such as pluck.

Mallets: Mallets are available in different sizes and in varying degrees of hardness or density. (See chapter 2.) Choose a mallet that will produce approximately the same timbre as the clapper head on the soft setting. There are two symbols used to indicate the use of mallets on bells:

+ The + with a dot beneath it indicates that the bell is resting on a padded table. Using a mallet of the proper size, weight and hardness, the bell is struck on the outside of the casting near the lip of the bell (at approximately the same place as the clapper strikes the inside of the bell).

+ The + alone indicates that the bell is held by the handle (suspended) and struck with a mallet as described above. Bells sounded in this manner usually are not damped.

WARNING: It is extremely important that a mallet of the proper hardness and density be used to strike any bell. Improper use of mallets may damage the bell casting. (See chapter 2.)

There are other ringing techniques, which you will encounter in music that is beyond the beginning level. The American Guild of English Handbell Ringers publishes a handbell notation brochure that may be obtained from the national office. (See chapter 16 for the AGEHR address and phone numbers.) This pamphlet lists all the notational symbols currently in use, gives the name and meaning of each symbol, and gives a brief description of how the technique is to be executed.

Shelly Ringing

There is one common and relatively simple ringing technique that might be useful to you even in the early stages of your bell choir's development. This technique is called Shelly ringing. It requires the ringer to hold and simultaneously ring two bells in one hand. Normally, both bells are relatively small bells, although ringers with large hands can use the technique on medium-size bells.

Follow these steps in learning this technique:

♪ Place two bells on the table, one handle over the other, to form a right angle. (The right angle will become more of an X when the bells are in-hand.)

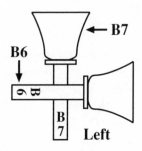

Left

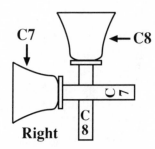

Right

♪ When this is done, the letter names on both handles should be up or where the ringer can see them. If the bells are adjusted so there is uneven tension on the clapper restraining springs, the manufacturer's logos on both handles should also be up or where the ringer can see them. (See chapter 7.)

♪ With either hand, grasp both bells in a clawlike manner, having the index finger between the bells, beneath the handguard at the top crossing of the X.

♪ Once in the ringer's hand, the clappers of the bells will both move in the same direction, forward and backward as in the basic ringing stroke.

♪ With a snap of the wrist, the ringer can cause both bells to ring simultaneously.

♪ This is a very helpful technique for ringing octaves. It is especially useful for pairing and Shelly ringing E6 and above, each bell being paired with the bell of the same name in the 7 octave. E6 would be paired with E7; F6 paired with F7; and similarly through C7 paired with C8 (for five octaves of bells).

Whether or not your ringers ever need to Shelly ring will depend on the bell assignments you make. In addition to being a ringing technique, it is also an assignment device that will prove more and more useful as the ringers progress and the music becomes more difficult.

Chapter Ten
Rehearsal Techniques

Before worrying about how to rehearse, decide when and how long the choir will rehearse. Scheduling is very important if you expect to get the commitment you need from the group. Check the church calendar and the school calendar(s) so you do not set a rehearsal time that will conflict with the ringers' existing schedules. Find a day of the week and a rehearsal time that are acceptable to you and to the number of ringers you need to organize a bell choir. Unless you are working with a children's bell choir that is a part of another music activity (and this would necessitate a shorter rehearsal time), I would recommend a rehearsal of forty-five minutes to one hour, even for beginning children's choirs. For youth and adult rehearsals, an hour would be the minimum. As youth and adult ringers progress, you might want to lengthen the time, but for most children's bell choirs, an hour rehearsal is sufficient. With all choirs, honor the time frame and begin on time and end on time.

From a musical standpoint, you will want to use the rehearsal time wisely, but you must also be aware of the need for group building and interaction among the ringers. Let the ringers know that the time to visit is before rehearsal, after rehearsal, or while changing music and bells. Let them know that you will not accept talking and visiting while the bell choir is rehearsing. Make it clear that when you talk, they listen, then be certain you have something worthwhile to say! Be concise in what you have to say, give instructions once, and do not let the ringers get in the habit of not paying attention because they know you will repeat your instructions one or more times.

Some directors like to use exercises or warm-up drills to begin each rehearsal. If you choose to do this, there are some excellent printed materials and collections that you can purchase. Personally I prefer to begin a rehearsal with a familiar piece of music that is relatively easy for the group. This might be something new to the group but not difficult for them, but more often it would be a piece of music they have rehearsed and know fairly well. If I want to use some type of exercise or drill to begin the rehearsal, I usually create it from something in the choir's repertoire. It is helpful to create an exercise from problem spots within the music the ringers will be rehearsing.

Working Out Problems Within the Music

Introducing a piece of music by ringing it from beginning to end without stopping is seldom constructive use of rehearsal time. Ringers need time to work out bell changes and any adjustments required to go from one ringing technique to another. Allow your ringers the time necessary to think about and work through the changes required in each new piece of music.

Good habits ringers should develop include:

- Always observe dynamic markings, even the first time the music is rung.
- Make music, do not just ring notes!
- Learn to count the music correctly, counting aloud and verbalizing rhythms when necessary.

Three Times and It Is a Habit

A wise piano teacher once told me, "Do something three times and it becomes a habit." Do not let mistakes continue or they will become habits. On the other hand, three times correctly can make a good habit! When my choirs have difficulty with a short passage, we isolate it and rehearse it until we can ring it correctly three times in a row. If we do it right twice and make a mistake the third time, we are back to zero and have to start over. The wise director will learn when to dwell on a problem and when not to make an issue of it. Do not let a ringer get uptight about getting his or her part right. If that happens, it is probably best to move on and rehearse something else. Address the problem passage in a future rehearsal.

Rhythmic Problems

I often tell my ringers, "If you cannot count it correctly, you cannot ring it correctly." Even if they can count it correctly, ringing it correctly may take more time! Here are some rhythmic games, drills, or exercises that will help the ringers work out rhythmic difficulties within their assignments:

- Count the rhythm of the entire passage aloud.
- Count aloud only on the counts that they will ring.

For those having problems ringing on the offbeats (the "ands"):

- Have them use one free hand to keep the beat and use the bell in the other hand to ring the "ands."
- Have them turn one bell sideways in one hand (so it will not ring); move that bell silently to keep the beat; ring the "ands" with the bell in the other hand.

Why Did I Stop?

Teach your ringers to listen to what is going on around them and become aware of whether or not the music is being rung correctly. When you stop the music before the end of the piece, ask them to tell you why you stopped. Ask them to identify the problem in general terms or by specific examples. After the ringers have identified the problem, repeat the passage and ask them if it was rung correctly this time. Teach them to become good listeners. When you ask the ringers to identify a problem, do not let them blame or correct another ringer. This is not an opportunity to be tattletales or a time for confessions! Sometimes ringers will confess their mistakes, but make them keep their confessions short and simple. Also let them know that when a ringer needs to be corrected, you will do the correcting. This prevents ringers from getting angry with other ringers!

Where Are We? REVIEW '99   FACE

Even the best of us get lost at times, but we do not have to stay lost. Teach your ringers to look and listen for things that will help them find their place in the music. Show them how to look and listen for:

♪ A cue or clue from the director
♪ Long note values where all the movement stops
♪ Changes from measures of quarter notes to measures of eighth notes
♪ Familiar rhythmic patterns
♪ Familiar melodic patterns and how they appear in the music
♪ Fermatas (holds)
♪ Different ringing techniques such as pluck, shake, swing, and so on
♪ A measure-number clue from a neighbor SAY: MEASURE

Rehearsing Changes Between Pieces of Music

Beginners especially need time to work out the details of moving from one piece of music to another. Some of the changes that have to be made include:

♪ Turning to the new piece of music
♪ Moving from one ringing position to another
♪ Organizing the bells assigned to a ringing position—setting the table plan
♪ Returning floater bells
♪ Getting new floater bells
♪ Getting mallets

♪ Thinking about the new piece of music and what will be
    required of the ringer
When preparing the choir to ring in worship or concert, rehearse
the pieces in the order in which they will be rung and rehearse
changing from one piece of music to the next. Have the group
make the changes as quickly and as quietly as possible. Do not
make last-minute changes in your instructions or plans, especially
when working with children.

Variety Within the Rehearsal

Keep the rehearsal moving, interesting, and productive.
Rehearse music that offers a change in tempo, level of difficulty,
and musical style. Determine which part of the rehearsal is the
most conducive for the group to work on their most difficult
piece(s). Some experts recommend presenting the music that
requires the most concentration about twenty minutes into the
rehearsal time. I have found that this varies from choir to choir
and age level to age level. With children, difficult or challenging
pieces often need to come early in the rehearsal, perhaps immediately after warming up on something familiar. End the rehearsal
by ringing a piece of music that will give the choir a feeling of
accomplishment. We always conclude our rehearsals with prayer.
Some rehearsals are wonderful. Others make you want to say,
"I will never go back!" but you know you will! If you feel that
things did not go well, ask yourself, "Why? What did I do wrong?
How can I improve?" When you have your answers, add them to
your list of things I learned after it was too late! Accept the chal-
lenge to make the next rehearsal better.

Chapter Eleven
Bells in Worship

From the very first time ringers participate in a worship service as a choir, they must know that they are not there to perform, but rather to lead in worship. The choirs, especially children's choirs, must be taught how to behave in worship; when, where, and how to move within the service; and how to serve as worship leaders.

Sharing with the congregation the new ministry of music through handbells is very important, but the choir must be well prepared before you schedule them to participate in a worship service. If the handbell program is new to the church, the congregation might need to be prepared to hear and receive the handbell music as part of worship. They, too, need to claim ownership of and give support to this new ministry of their church.

I cannot emphasize enough the importance of having the bell choir musically well prepared for their first appearance in a worship service (or on any program, for that matter!). Some people (particularly some adults) are hesitant to do anything before a group of people, so ringing for the first time can be very frightening for them. One of our adult ringers became so ill every time she rang in public that she had to seek medical help and eventually had to quit the bell choir! Such an extreme case does not happen often, but be sensitive to the nervousness of all first-time ringers, especially the adult ringers. Usually, with time and ringing experience, ringers will overcome their extreme nervousness. A member of one adult bell choir had the courage to admit that the group had finally learned to "breathe and ring at the same time!"

Uses of Bells in Worship

The following are the most obvious places in the service to use music from the choir's repertoire:

♪ Prelude
♪ Anthem
♪ Offertory
♪ Postlude

Having the choir ring all four of these portions of the service might be too much, but a combination of two or three would be good. Ringing these musical portions of the service is probably the easiest way to incorporate bells in the worship service because you can select suitable music that the choir already knows well. When the bell choir presents the music for one of these four elements of the service, it rings as an entity and not as part of a vocal choir, an instrumental group, or as part of the congregational singing. For the choir's first experience participating in worship, I always have them ring the prelude and the anthem because these are the least stressful, yet very important, parts of the service for which the choir can assume responsibility and give leadership.

Hymn Accompaniments/Descants

You can purchase handbell arrangements written especially for use in accompanying congregational singing. To be heard above the voices, the arrangements should make more use of the high bells than of the low bells. Congregational singing may also be added to handbell arrangements of familiar hymn tunes. Be certain the bell arrangement is in a singable key!

Anthem Accompaniments and Descants

Use the bell choir instead of the piano or organ to accompany the singing choir. The bell choir may ring a descant to the choir's anthem. If the descant requires only a few bells, these may be distributed to and rung by various members of the singing choir.

Introit, Benediction, and Other Responses

Music selected for these portions of the service may include:
♪ A composition written for this purpose

♪ An excerpt taken from a piece rung in its entirety at another time in the service

♪ An excerpt from music in the choir's repertoire but not otherwise used in the service

Processionals

Processionals may include:

♪ Music written especially for handbell processionals

♪ An excerpt taken from a composition in the choir's repertoire

Often the first four to eight measures of the bell choir's prelude can be memorized and rung as a processional. When the choir has reached its place behind the bell tables, at the director's signal, the ringers continue past the memorized portion of music and the processional becomes the prelude.

Random Ringing

Random ringing may be done with the bell choir already in its place in the sanctuary, or ringers may be stationed at selected places within the sanctuary or just outside the sanctuary. In both instances, each ringer holds two bells, and the ringing begins softly with just a few bells being rung at random. If the random ringing is done as a processional, as the ringers move into the sanctuary and into position at the bell tables, more bells are added, the tempo increases, and the music crescendos. When the choir is in place (or if the choir did not process, when the allotted time is over), the director signals for the damping of all bells except the ones in a previously determined chord—the chord that will lead into the hymn, call to worship, or the next musical portion of the service.

Handbells with Instruments

Options include:

♪ A handbell composition that includes a solo instrument

♪ A composition for handbell choir and keyboard instrument
♪ A composition for handbell choir and brass choir
♪ A composition that includes some combination of bells, brass, organ, choir, and congregation

Handbells and the Spoken Word

The combination of narrator and handbell choir is quite effective. Options within this category include:
♪ Scripture and a non-hymn-based handbell composition
♪ Handbell setting of a hymn tune to which an appropriate scriptural narration has been added
♪ Combination of a hymn-based handbell arrangement, solo instrument, and scriptural narration
This is in no way an exhaustive list of ways handbells may be used in worship, but I have tried to mention simple ways that would allow even beginning bell choirs to participate in worship. Use your imagination, be creative, and find new ways to use handbells in your church's worship services.

Rehearsing the Logistics of Ringing in Worship

Not only do ringers need to be musically well prepared for their participation in worship, they also need to be well prepared for the moves they will need to make during the service. Giving attention to the following details will help the service flow smoothly.
♪ Rehearse in the worship area.
  ♪ The bell table configuration may be different from that in the rehearsal room.
  ♪ The acoustics will be different.
♪ Rehearse bell changes in the worship area.
♪ Rehearse moves to and from the tables in the worship area.
  ♪ Have ringers move at an appropriate part of the service when the movement will be least conspicuous.

♪ Do not allow "dead time" while changes and moves are being made.

♪ Do not allow the bell choir's movements to stop the flow of the service.

The music the ringers present is an important part of their contribution to the worship service, but the way they conduct themselves before, during, and after the service is equally important. Ringers are seen before they are heard! Their attitudes during the service, as well as the music they ring, may be the only sermon some worshipers hear that day. This is an awesome responsibility! Help them accept it so that they may become effective worship leaders.

Chapter Twelve
Bell Choir Clothing

R ingers are seen before they are heard. None of us have a
second chance to make a good first impression! When
selecting clothing for the bell choir to wear, keep the following in mind:

♪ The ringers should look nice and be well dressed.

♪ The choir should have a uniform appearance.

♪ The clothing should be appropriate for worship or concert.

♪ The purchase of bell choir clothing should not place a financial burden on the ringers or their families.

♪ Ringers come in all sizes and shapes!

♪ The color and style of clothing should be flattering to all ringers.

♪ Choose a clothing style that is not overwhelming when worn
by all the ringers. What looks great on one ringer may be too
much when worn by ten or twelve!

♪ Choose clothing that can be replaced as ringers grow.

Keeping all those factors in mind, the following are some types of
clothing that have been chosen by many bell choirs.

Robes: If the church's budget allows, robes may be the ideal solu-
tion to what the bell choir will wear. They are always appropriate for worship and in most instances would be appropriate for
concert. (They do need special care if they are taken on tour
with the choir.) Regular choir robes, perhaps shared with the
vocal choirs, are fine for children and beginning or intermediate bell choirs, but the loose sleeves may cause problems for
advanced choirs. Robes with cuffed sleeves are ideal, even for
the most advanced choirs.

Formal attire: Some youth and adult choirs are now wearing tuxe-
do shirts, pants, cummerbunds, and ties for their ringing outfits.
This would certainly be suitable clothing for the concert setting, but it could become an expensive investment. It might or
might not be acceptable in the worship setting.

Identifying outfits: If chosen wisely with regard to color, fabric, and style, the following would be appropriate wearing apparel for worship or concert:

♪ Skirt/blouse or shirt/tie/and dress pants

♪ Knit shirts and slacks/skirt

♪ Vests or tunics worn with skirts/blouses and shirt/slacks

After years of trying to decide on suitable wearing apparel for our choirs, including having a "wear your Sunday-go-to-meeting clothes" policy, we have found the following clothing the most practical, economical, attractive, and acceptable to our youth ringers. (Our children's choirs and adult ringers wear robes.)

Boys:

♪ Navy slacks, navy tie, long-sleeved white shirt

♪ Dark dress shoes and socks

Girls:

♪ Navy skirts (style and material of the ringer's choosing)

♪ Long-sleeved white blouse

♪ A dressy, but easy-care fabric

♪ Open neck, notched collar

♪ A simple, easy-to-match style

♪ Available in a wide variety of sizes

♪ Available through a catalogue

♪ Dark hose and dress shoes

Each ringer also wears a St. James Ringers stole, which is similar to a minister's stole or the ringer's stoles that can be found in choir robe catalogues. We have made these stoles from navy felt, outlined them with red middy braid, and added a white felt logo at each end of the stole. The stoles are owned by the church and are part of the bell choir equipment.

Whatever style of clothing is chosen, it should be suitable to the occasions for which the bell choir will be ringing. It should be comfortable to wear and roomy enough to allow the ringers the necessary freedom of movement. The girls' skirts should be long enough so that, when the choir is ringing on a platform, the audience or congregation will not be singing, "Do you see what I see?"

Chapter Thirteen
What the Handbell Ringing Experience Should Be

There is so much more to bell choir than just ringing a handbell! There are Christian values to be taught. There are abundant opportunities to:

♪ Learn the value of teamwork
♪ Make lifelong friendships
♪ Learn the importance of commitment
♪ Develop self-discipline
♪ Witness to the church and the community through music

By participating in a bell choir, ringers can be a part of a group that reaches a performance level that few ringers would reach as solo performers on any instrument. Most of us are not instrumentalists or soloists of concert caliber, yet as members of an advanced bell choir, we can be part of a high caliber group.

1. Ringing in a bell choir should be an enjoyable experience.
Although everyone should have a good time, there still must be discipline in every rehearsal. With children, and sometimes with youth, the discipline will be director imposed, but as the ringers grow and mature, they must develop a high degree of self-discipline. Learning must take place in every rehearsal. You should expect and accept nothing but the ringers' best. Be realistic in your expectations, but expect mistakes. We all make them, even handbell directors! Help your ringers realize that every job that is done is a self-portrait of the person who did it. Teach them to autograph their work with excellence!

2. Use kindness rather than criticism. Be demanding but not demeaning.
♪ Find something to compliment.
♪ Be quicker to compliment than to criticize.
♪ Be positive.

♪ Be consistent.

♪ Be kind.

♪ Be fair.

Everyone responds to kindness and everyone likes to receive a well-deserved compliment. Ringers will live up (or down) to what you expect of them. They know when they have done a poor job or have given less than their best. When you treat your ringers in the ways listed above, as you would want them to treat you, they will work harder for you than if you constantly find fault and criticize them. Yes, you as the director must correct the ringers, but do so in a positive, encouraging way. Do not let ringers correct other ringers!

3. **It is difficult to leave problems outside the rehearsal room door.** As directors, none of us know what problems the ringers have faced that day at home, at school, or at work. Many of them are dealing with the insecurities they feel in other areas of their lives. Sometimes the church is literally the only place where they feel safe. Sometimes it is the only place where they feel wanted, needed, and loved. The last thing they need is to be fussed at and scolded during rehearsals! Make every rehearsal an affirmation of each ringer's worth and importance.

4. **Bell ringing should be a positive experience that ringers will always remember.** Most people, especially today's youth, do not realize how much they will miss bell choir until they are no longer part of a choir. As it is happening, they do not realize the important influence the bell choir is having on their lives. As the Jewish proverb expresses, "A joy is not fulfilled until it becomes a memory." Help the ringers develop an appreciation for good music. Help them develop a deep and abiding love for God and the church. Be a good role model for them. In everything you do, set a Christian example for them to follow.

Chapter Fourteen
Teaching Values

In chapter 1 and chapter 13, we enumerated specific values that we try to teach and instill in each of our ringers. The question remains, "How are these values taught?"

1. **Values are taught from day one and throughout the year.** Learning is a process, not an event. Therefore, when we teach our ringers, whether we are teaching music or Christian and moral values, our work begins at the first rehearsal and continues throughout the year(s).

2. **Values are taught by having respect for every individual.** Respect cannot be demanded. Respect must be earned. You must respect your ringers and you must earn their respect in return. Although you want the ringers to like you, it is far more important that they respect you. To quote Father George W. Tribou, rector of Catholic High School for Boys in Little Rock, Arkansas, "It is not important what a sixteen-year-old thinks of you, but it is important what he thinks of you when he is thirty-six."

3. **Values are taught by setting the right kind of example.** Ringers must know that you are not going to do anything un-christian or unprofessional. They must know that you are not going to behave in a way that would cause embarrassment to them or to you. They must know that, as adults, we know, respect, and abide by the rules just as we expect ringers to abide by the rules. In other words, there are no double standards!

4. **Values are taught by showing that we genuinely like and enjoy our work.** Let the ringers know that you are glad to be there and that you enjoy working with handbells. Let them know that you enjoy working with ringers and that you are especially glad to be working with them. Let your enthusiasm for your work be contagious!

The Rehearsal Setting

Earlier we discussed space and equipment needed in the hand-bell rehearsal room. These things are important, but the rehearsal room should also have a special feeling about it—a special atmosphere. When the ringers walk through the rehearsal room door, they should know that they are in a place where they will be safe. In today's world, safe can literally mean safe from the dangers of the outside world. Here is a place where rules are known and respected, where boundaries—reasonable boundaries—are set and honored, and where everyone knows the consequences of breaking the rules. The rules must be fair and they must be consistently enforced.

Consistency is an important element in the organization and functioning of a successful bell choir or handbell program. As directors, we must be consistent in what we say and do. We must not keep changing the rules or changing our mind once we have made a decision. We must be consistent in the way we behave and in what we expect of the ringers. Having rules, setting boundaries, and being consistent in their enforcement give the ringers a much-needed sense of security. Bell choir is not the place to be like Charlie Brown: wishy-washy!

The Open-Door Policy

Our ringers know that our door is always open to them. They can come in and talk or vent their frustrations from the day's events. Some come and do their homework while others come to discuss the latest happenings on their favorite soap operas! Spending a few informal minutes with the ringers each week allows them to get to know you as a person, not just as the choir director. All of the ringers know that they are welcome, that they are loved, and that they have worth as individuals. Experts have said that as our society becomes more high-tech it must also become more high-touch. Mutually given in the proper way, hugs can mean a lot to the ringers. It is amazing how many teenagers, boys as well as girls, will line up after rehearsal for their weekly hug!

Support from the Minister and from the Church

Several years ago my husband and I made a difficult decision that could have cost us our jobs. For many valid reasons, we chose not to promote into the "top" bell choir the daughters of two of the church's "founding families." Our minister supported our decision and our reasons for making it even though it meant that one family joined another church. I hope that you, as a handbell director, will have this kind of support from your minister. The story does have a happy ending, though! Both ringers are now grown and have come back to St. James. They are active in the life of the church; one is still ringing handbells!

Setting high standards may not be so difficult, but abiding by them can be! Sometimes it would have been so much easier to have relaxed the rules, to have looked the other way, to have given in, but we chose not to compromise our standards! The St. James music ministry is now reaping the benefits of having set and upheld high standards. Ringers and former students who were taught to embrace these standards are now becoming parents (even parents of ringers!). They realize that the values learned in bell choir have played an important part in their lives and they are teaching these values to their children. They know how much the handbell choir experience meant to them, and they want their children to have the same opportunities.

Now It's Your Turn!

Each individual must find his or her own way of working with people. None of us can copy what works for someone else and expect it to work equally well for us. However, each of us can assimilate and adapt ideas, making them fit our own personality and needs. The ideas and concepts expressed in this book are not necessarily right or wrong, they are opinions—my opinions—about things that, for us, have worked well. Take whatever ideas you think will be useful to you in your ministry and adapt them to fit your specific situation.

In your work as a church musician, remember:

♪ Your work is not a job, it is a way of life.

♪ The people you work with are more important than the music. Put the people first and the music will happen.

♪ With God's help, the best is yet to be.

Chapter Fifteen
Helpful Handbell Hints

HINT #1: Make tabs from cellophane tape or masking tape to help the ringers turn pages. (I recently saw a group of adult ringers make turning tabs from Post-it Notes.) Stagger the tabs so they can be easily grasped.

HINT #2: Adult ringers may want to provide their own small metal binder clips, which they attach to the music and use for page-turning tabs. Each ringer should attach the tabs to his or her own music before ringing and remove them after the rehearsal, worship service, or concert.

HINT #3: If the director allows, to facilitate page turning, printed music can be cut horizontally at selected places on selected pages. This allows the ringer to turn the page at a convenient time when the turn at the end of the page is inconvenient.

HINT #4: Cotton garden gloves make excellent practice gloves.

HINT #5: If the church purchases white performance gloves for ringers (and keeps the gloves as part of the bell equipment), here is an easy way to identify the size of each glove:
  ♪ Choose a specific color permanent marker to use on each size glove.
  ♪ At the upper edge of the glove (palm side), mark a colored dot on all the right-hand gloves of that size and a colored line on all the left hand gloves of that size.
  ♪ Finding gloves, one with a dot and one with a line of the same color, will assure the ringer of having a pair of gloves.

HINT #6: If ringers complain that blisters are beginning to form on their hands, have them place the open center of a corn pad over the point of irritation.

HINT #7: The *counting only* can be copied onto printed music by using the copy machine. Here is how to do this:
  ♪ Carefully place a piece of onion-skin paper over the page of printed music.

♪ Tape two pieces of onion-skin paper together to cover a two-page spread of music.

♪ With a felt-tip marker, on the onion-skin paper, write the desired counting under the notes or in the center of the grand staff. This is easy to do because the paper is transparent.

♪ Place the onion-skin paper (with the counting written on it) in the copy machine as the original material that is to be copied. Place it carefully, matching indications for the edges of the paper.

♪ Put the printed music in the copy machine bin where you would normally place the blank sheets of paper.

♪ Print. Only the counting will be copied onto the printed music!

HINT #8: Vinyl sheet protectors have several possible uses:

♪ To protect the music from wear and tear (the music must be cut so that individual pages can be inserted into the protectors).

♪ To allow markings to be placed on the protectors instead of on the music (color-coding markings can be written on the vinyl and erased as needed, or by leaving the music in the protectors, the marked music can be reused).

Chapter Sixteen
Resource Materials and Information

The American Guild of English Handbell Ringers, Inc.

Uniting People Through a Musical Art

The American Guild of English Handbell Ringers, Inc. (AGEHR) is a nonprofit organization established in 1954 to promote the art of English handbell ringing. The national office is located in Dayton, Ohio.

AGEHR, Inc.
1055 East Centerville Station Road
Dayton, OH 45459-5503
1-800-878-5459
1-513-438-0085
FAX 1-513-438-0434

Office hours are 8:00 to 5:00, Monday through Thursday, and 8:00 to 4:30 (Eastern Time) on Fridays.

The AGEHR strives for musical excellence through:

   ♪ National events that bring together ringers and directors from all over the world
   ♪ Area events that bring together ringers and directors from limited geographic regions

♪ Publications
♪ Exchanges of ideas related to all aspects of ringing, writing, and conducting handbell music

All members living in the United States or Canada are "resident" members; all other members are considered "foreign" members who may participate in AGEHR events and share in all the privileges of membership except eligibility for holding a national office.

I believe that membership in AGEHR is a must for handbell directors and is a wonderful option for ringers. Churches, schools, and other organizations that sponsor handbell choirs should be members of AGEHR because of the opportunities and resources afforded its members.

Each member has the opportunity to:

♪ Attend local, area, and national events
♪ Network with other handbell professionals
♪ Receive a subscription to *Overtones,* the official publication of AGEHR, Inc.
♪ Receive the annual roster
♪ Receive the newsletter from the member's home area
♪ Purchase and wear the AGEHR membership insignia
♪ Receive music and catalogues from Handbell Industry Council members
♪ Stand for election or be appointed to an area or national office
♪ Vote in all area and national elections and attend business meetings
♪ Ringers in a member's choir or ringer members have all the privileges listed above except the right to vote, to hold office, and receive music from Handbell Industry Council members

AGEHR Membership Categories
Regular Member: For both individual and choir/group
Ringer: Must belong to choir of a regular member
Senior Citizen: An individual membership—may not represent a group

Full-time Students: An individual membership—may not represent a group
Sterling
Platinum
Business/Commercial

Membership categories and dues are determined by the National Board of Directors of AGEHR, Inc. Consult the national office in Dayton, Ohio for the latest information.

Canadian and overseas members should add $10 to the dues for all membership categories.

The following is not intended to be an exhaustive list of books and materials for the beginning handbell choir. However, these are materials that you may find useful to you in your work. Directors should always search for new materials and keep themselves well informed regarding the latest publications.

Books for Further Reading

AGEHR PAMPHLETS. Various subjects. Various authors.

A Beginner's Book of Handbell Music for Two Octaves. Sallie Lloyd. Beckenhorst. HBC-1.
Bell, Book, and Ringer. Martha Lynn Thompson. Flammer HL-5144.
Handbell Ringing. Robert Ivey. Agape 1838.
Joyfully Ring. Donald E. Allured. Broadman 4574-15.
Learning to Ring Series (Director's Manual). Van Valey and Berry. Lorenz HB 200.
Musical Excellence in Handbells. Donald E. Allured. Broadman 0-8054-3304-X.
Mastering Musicianship in Handbells. Donald E. Allured. Broadman 4591-54.

Collections of Music for the Beginning Bell Choir

Ready to Ring. Thompson/Callahan. Agape 1110 (2-5 octaves).
Ready to Ring II. Thompson/Callahan. Agape 1168 (2 octaves).
Ready to Ring III. Thompson/Callahan. Agape 1198 (3-5 octaves).

Ready to Ring for Christmas. Thompson/Callahan. Agape 1352 (2 octaves).
Ready to Ring for Christmas. Thompson/Callahan. Agape 1353 (3-5 octaves).

Begin to Ring 2. Thompson/Callahan. Agape 1242 (2 octaves).
Begin to Ring 3. Thompson/Callahan. Agape 1243 (3 octaves).

Clapper Classics (2). Thompson/Callahan. Agape 1253 (3 octaves).

Clapper Classics (3). Thompson/Callahan. Agape 1254 (3 octaves).
More Clapper Classics. Thompson/Callahan. Agape 1276 (3 octaves).

Keyrings (Ringer). Thompson/Callahan. Agape 1347 (3 octaves).
Keyrings (Director). Thompson/Callahan Agape 1348 (3 octaves).
More Keyrings (Ringer). Thompson/Callahan. Agape 1579 (3 octaves).
More Keyrings. (Director). Thompson/Callahan. Agape 1601 (3 octaves).

Classic Rings. Thompson/Callahan. Agape 1662 (3 octaves).

Rhythm and Bells. Martha Lynn Thompson. Agape 1772 (2-3 octaves).

Time to Ring. Martha Lynn Thompson. Agape 1873 (3 octaves).

Ring Praise I. Wayne Kerr. Concordia 97-5900 (3 octaves).
Ring Praise II. Wayne Kerr. Concordia 97-6016 (3 octaves).
Ringing for the First Time (Ringer). Linda McKechnie. Flammer HL-5233 (3 octaves).
Ringing for the First Time (Director). Linda McKechnie. Flammer HL-5232 (3 octaves).

Music for the Beginning Bell Choir. Linda McKechnie. Choristers Guild CGBK-57 (3 octaves).

Ringing Basics. Beverly Simpson. Flammer HL 5231.

Making Music with Choir Chime Instruments. Paul Rosene. Agape 1159.

Let the Children Ring. Gerald Armstrong. Broadman 4591-04